The Other Side of Healing

Remembering My Journey to Healing

Tichamingo White

May God be
with you & bless
you always !
& Shalom
Tichamingo

COPYRIGHT 2021 by Tichamingo White

Cover Illustration by Charmaine Butler

Table of Contents

INTRODUCTION

My story is one that many people can't handle, and that is ok with me because it is just that, my story. Everyone has a story, and no two people will have the same take away from their unique experience. That is one funny thing about life, you can't tell my story, but you can share how my story helped you. We all go through situations and circumstances that leave us in a state of trying to understand, "what's going on," or "why me." My experience had me stuck on stupid trying to figure out, what's really going on! My upbringing and background wouldn't allow me to probe the, "why me" so I found myself embracing the, "why not me?" Given the fact that what I have been through, really isn't for me anyway, but it is designed to help other people get to a better understanding of what they may be dealing with right now. The question then becomes, "am I willing to expose my personal thoughts about what has occurred in my life, in order to help others?" This requires vulnerability on a level that most people aren't ready for. For every positive word of encouragement, you receive, there will always be ten negative remarks that have the potential to cut deep...let's face it, that is the world in which we live. The true test or strength of what we experience is seen only when we share with others. My desire with sharing my story is simple; if I can live in a healthier place, anyone can.

The Other Side of Healing

This book has been floating in my head for many years, this is probably the second time I have been inclined to pull it out of my head into book format. There has been at least twelve years that has gone by from when I had the thought to share my experience, with the actual writing of it. Today more than ever I'm ready to drop the pen to the pad and flow freely into the journey from how my life was rudely interrupted with mental health, a subject that was unheard of in my life and world. This book will allow you to see my personal introduction with issues associated with the stigma of mental health and all the in between with coming to grip with such a debilitating condition, and yet maintaining a positive push and determination to stay healthy.

I would like to extend a warm thank you to everyone in my support system, I truly appreciate each and every one of you. To my son, thank you for being my hope that held me together during my most vulnerable points of this journey.

If what I am experiencing now is what healing looks like, then what I went through to get where I am today was a place that was frightening and what I call the Other side of Healing.

I pray that my story leads you all on a pathway that helps you become more understanding of all of the millions of people who suffer in silence daily with mental health conditions; I love and appreciation you.

CHAPTER 1

FIRST THINGS FIRST

My background is humble, or in some circles viewed as not having much as far as stuff, or worldly possessions go. What I did have was a lot of love, and from my experience many people don't have that growing up. For that I am most grateful. Love has been the most grounding aspect of who I am for various reasons.

I grew up in a family that consisted of my mom, two older sisters and in my formative years a stepdad, that played an interesting role in my life at that time. I was born in Ohio, and my family moved when I was four years old to California.

Growing up in California gave me a good sense of wellbeing and shaped me into a young lady that had confidence and a healthy image of myself. I had three older brothers on my mom's side and siblings or sibling on my biological father's side that I did not grow up with, and really until I became an adult, didn't know much about. I grew up as the baby girl in my family. Sibling order plays a vital role in people's life; however, many people are truly unaware of how it impacts your life until someone brings it to your attention. For me, I received a lot of attention and was the object of affection from people in my life. I never sought-after attention, nor did I do anything to get attention or affection from others. I thought every family showed love and attention to their children because of how my family supported me. It wasn't until I matured that I realized that wasn't the case for many. I remember my mother sending my sisters and I to church, at a time she wasn't going herself. Then my mother started attending church and later became a minister and pastor. We had bible study every night in this older lady's house, where we learned how to study the bible, and how real God is. That was what we did and how I became introduced to my experience with the Lord. I witnessed God use my mother to the extent of people being healed right before my eyes. My middle big sister broke her arm in two places when we were younger, arm wrestling with our godbrother that had some training in martial arts. She had a cast placed to set her arm, however when the cast came off, her arm wouldn't extend like it had before the injury. My mother prayed for my sister and touched her arm and it straighten and went back to where it had been prior to the wrestling accident. It was during this time of my elementary years that I concluded that God was powerful and could use whatever He needed to get His point across.

I learned a lot through observation as a child, my mother could talk to me, and I would do right...I don't recall ever getting a whooping. That is saying a lot considering I grew up in the era where kids got whooping's from their family and could get whipped from a neighbor also. I was good in school and earned good grades. I enjoyed learning. During my elementary school days, I played around with learning the piano, speaking Spanish, and I developed an appreciation for American sign language.

I consider myself to be the ruff and prissy type. I would collect hot wheels and exchange them with the boys and collect and play dolls with the girls I knew. It was no thing for me to hop on the back of a bike and hang out with the fellas, then turn around and play jacks with my friend girls. I was extremely independent of others at times, I would get out of elementary school and canvas my neighbor for hours collecting aluminum cans or selling candy bars. I bought my first bike off the money I made. There was this boy that I went to school with, he was bad. I remember having to fight this boy every day after school in the sixth grade. The last fight I remember having with him, one of the other boys at my school held the bad boy down and told me to run. I decided before I ran that I would turn on a near- by water hose and drench this bad boy, then I took off running toward where I lived. Once I got to where I lived, I stopped running and waited for the bad boy to catch up with me and we went toe to toe blow for blow. This was the way of life in the hood, you didn't have the option to avoid bullies, you knuckled up and went for broke, but you lived to tell the story.

This was a rite of passage of sorts, I guess. I didn't pick fights, but I wasn't afraid to thump if I had too. Another one of my favorite pastimes was listening to music and singing. It was early on that I discovered my enjoyment of putting words together through poetry.

3

I would create my own poems and sometimes reflect on poems that I came across. I sang in the choir in the little storefront church I attended growing up and I have fond memories of going to music workshops where I witness the great Dr. Mattie Moss Clark share her expertise in gospel music. This was the fabric of my childhood, the sense of community was strong, and people really looked out for one another. My mother is from the south originally, and I have lived out southern hospitality to the fullest. The city I grew up in, is a military port and my family would embrace those individuals that were far from home and make them feel accepted and give them a source of support away from home. On any given day there was always at least four to five extra plates for dinner in our home. We never made people feel unwanted, even if you were invited over and you brought extra people, we didn't know with you...everyone was included and there was always enough food to go around.

My life in California wasn't tainted with all roses, there was ugliness lurking all around me, however many of the devastating events that have plagued so many I didn't become a victim of. I heard stories, even seen troubling situations occur; somehow, I was able to get through it all without much scaring.

I remember my oldest sister meeting life threating gang situations. In the part of town, we lived in, it was heavily populated with the gang called, "crips." My sister went to school during a time where the Mexican gangs were feuding with the crips, and she was involved with a big riot that broke out at her school. It was my sister, and two of her friends, one male and the other female fighting back - to- back against at least twenty people. It was a tough time to live in the hood, many of the gangs that people read about were at the initial stages of development and we lived right in the heart of the activity that crept into the urban lifestyle. I imagine that circumstances could have played out unfavorable for my sister, however she came out of this event with her life.

Life appeared from my eyes, to be not that complicated. I guess my view was limited to my experience, of which during this period I didn't have much of. One aspect of my background seemed to be unknown to me, was any real education or information about black awareness. I didn't grow up with learning about black people and their struggles nor their accomplishments. I mean, don't get me wrong my elementary school talked about Martin Luther King Junior, and possibly Fredrick Douglas...but that was it at school. I don't remember my mother sharing any information regarding the subject matter at home either. It wasn't until I took my first college course that I began to learn about black people and the life in which we have lived. I find this to be ever so interesting. I have never been told that I was black, but I knew I was. I was never prepped nor primed for or against anyone. I lived in a world that was a melting pot that consisted and thrived of individuals that came from a variety of different backgrounds, however my mother always instilled in me to treat people right and you will be treated right in return. This has been true from the stand point that you are being treated right, may not always come from the people you are doing right by, nonetheless; you will get back what you put out.

I have always been a teacher of sorts, as long as I can remember. When I was in elementary, there was a group home next to the apartment my family lived in, for troubled teen age boys. The group home had been relocated, and there were schoolbooks that were left behind. I gathered all the books I could carry and went back at least three times and sorted through the books and came out with a surplus of teaching material. This sparked my teaching career, and I was off to share my knowledge with all that would listen! I began to tutor my peers and older kids in the neighbor in English, Math, and Science. On one occasion one of my friends wanted to be the teacher, and I quickly agreed then I put away all my school supplies and instructed my friend to teach with her supplies. My friend didn't have any school supplies, and I exclaimed, "well I guess you can't teach until you have supplies!" This approach and mindset would play out as my personal passion in life, a hidden talent of sorts. I have always found great reward in aiding people with a better understanding of any subject that was abstract to them, or could it be the fact of me having the supplies to get the job done? Teaching has proving to be a form of therapy for me. I have discovered that as I engage in the preparation needed to teach a lesson, I benefit twice; once while doing research and secondly by delivering the information. There is something about teaching that opens my mind to believe in the ability of making a change, even if the process renders you speechless and unable to mask the disparity of people that catch on fast, and those that get lost in the toss. One of the saddest commentaries I have witnessed as a teacher has been when a person is unable to start the process of change through learning, due to not having the skill set to accomplish the task. As a teacher, the solution to this equation, seems to be to aid the individual with practical means of getting around this dilemma...in theory this works; however, in reality what I have seen looks more like this: you can attempt to teach all you like, until your blue in the face; if a person doesn't possess the skill set to repeat, duplicate, or implement what they think you have taught...it unfortunately won't stick. What do you do then? Exactly, what to do is the question, however many people are in this situation for various reasons, which has more to do with how they are hard wired than anything else. For this cause, I continue to teach and strive to be of some sort of help, knowing that some wont, or can't be helped in the way I desire, but the offer to be of assistance remains true and genuine. My experience and introduction to teaching has been a running joke that I lovingly share about myself and find the humor of it to be a source of good conversation in social settings!

I can't share the background of my upbringing without including a few stories I have from living in Ohio prior to moving to

California as a child. One story deals with my biological father, although I don't have a memory of the events surrounding the details, my family has made me fully aware of how it all went down. My mom and dad had a causal connection that resulted in me being the byproduct of that encounter...they weren't involved for long, and outside of me being born, there wasn't much to it. My father lived the life he wanted, or should I say he lived out the life that he lived in...not much to say about the circumstances that causes a person to make choices that they have a hard time understanding, let alone trying to get from under those choices that ultimately lead to his demise. One thing I will say is that my father loved me and I him. No one can ever take that away from me. There have never been any ill feelings about or toward my father ever. I have always been the type of person to look past what a person may or may not be doing, and still see love, that is the only way I know to approach sensitive situations: with forgiveness and love, lots of it. My father came to my grandfather's house when I was a toddler and walked up to the porch and seen me through the screen and I went straight to him, he proceeded to leave without anyone inside the house knowing that he had been by there, and he took me with him. It wasn't long before my mom noticed that I wasn't in the living room where she had just left me. This is the earliest memory I have of my father, and I have always chuckled at this story, not sure why; but it is dear to me for some reason or another. That was the last time my dad seen me, and it would be at least forty-three years before I would have my own memories of my father, and we would see each other again. The other story that has been a very critical part of Ohio living, as a toddler; was the fire in an apartment building we lived in, that was the main reason we moved west.

We lived on the third floor of a building that also had a basement unit apartment. I don't know all of the details surrounding how the fire started, but I recall the fact of the fire being in the basement and reaching up to the third floor. The smoke was thick, and we could not breathe. My mom and our stepdad tried to wet blankets and put them over us to see if we could exit the building by the staircase. The cloud of black smoke prevented us from using the stairs, in a daze filled with adrenaline; my mom started busting out the windows with her bare hands, in our apartment to free us. Unfortunately, she had to make a lifesaving decision, we had to be thrown out of the third story window. I don't remember which of my two sisters or myself went out the window first, but I can still see that dark smoky hallway of that burning building as I write. I went into shock as I was place to the edge of the window and gently dropped out, as people on the ground level shouted for my mom to let go and they ensured her that they would catch me...the only thing that caught me was the ground. I remember that there was snow on the ground, yet I do not remember being cold. I went numb. I had to be every bit of 4 years old when this trauma occurred, and I can still smell the stench of the smoke in my nostrils, that is probably why I can't stand the smell of smoke today. My oldest sister is 4 years older than myself;

my middle sister is 2 years older; we all survived the fire with different outcomes. My stepdad sprained his leg. My mom jumped out the window holding her friends 1 year old in her arms. She broke her collar bone and bit a hole through her tongue. My oldest sister sprained her knee upon impact. My middle sister had a bump on her forehead. I had a cut on my upper thigh from the glass. In the midst of all of the drama and commotion associated with getting out of that burning building, my oldest sister and I were separated from my mom, stepdad, middle sister, and the toddler my mom had with her. They went to the hospital, and we ended up at someone's house. I was in a state of shock, which I'm uncertain if anyone realize it at the time. I stop talking. I don't remember for how long, but I do remember that this event caused me to internalize and suppress my emotions; or better yet, I had a difficult time emoting. I recognize it now, for what it is and how this event shaped me, however this is a recent discovery. It turned out that a few weeks went by before my oldest sister, and I were reunited with the rest of the family. I have this vivid picture of my mom's face, she was swollen; and I was afraid. My oldest sister clung onto me during our absence from the family, and she has proven to be a protector of me since then. I'm grateful that we made it out with our lives, however we all have borne unseen scars from this event.

I share this story because I have a place in my history where I can pinpoint a traumatic event, that played a key part of how the events affected me, that until I began writing...I was consciously unaware of; however subconsciously I have known that this was a forever, earth shaking and mountain moving experience for me. Here recently, I have learned that trauma can be debilitating if left unattended...therefore the ability to seek assistance with getting in front of the situation; by way of dealing with the ins and outs of it has proven to be a source of strength for me.

I have always sought-after resolve, in any given situation; so, I have over the years tried to educate myself on how to become wiser, and more apt to overcome barriers, and obstacles as they present themselves. It has been a long road of discoveries during my lifetime, some sad, glad, and most importantly necessary...or so it seems. If you take a poll and ask people if they now understand all of the previous mentioned discoveries on their pathway of life, I believe that most people would say that they don't know why the events occurred. I may not know the "why," but I am a well-rounded person as a result of what I have endured. If I decided to complain, that wouldn't strengthen me, but drain the drive to overcome out of me, so I choose to focus on becoming better, and not bitter.

I have nothing more to do, than to continue forward; despite circumstances, and situations. I will not become a part of the problem, but I will strive to make constant progression to a higher plain of healing the inner me.

CHAPTER 2

UPSIDE DOWN

My Mother was married to a younger man during the time I was in elementary school, as I got older, I realized that he was at least 18 years younger than her; I say that as a means of possibly understanding the devastating break up they had. The events surrounding the end of their relationship was based on lies, envy, and just plain old foolishness. It involved one of my Aunts, and a whole lot of crazy and bizarre behavior, to say the least (and that is putting it kindly). My stepdad ended up leaving the relationship, and headed for the military, which could have been a great move...going to the military that is. I conclude the whole experience as a sign of immaturity, that probably would not have occurred had he and my mother been wiser and apt to handle conflict in a manner that would have had a healthier outcome. Nevertheless, the events that occurred in our household impacted all of us for a lifetime.

There were nights, after the breakup I would hear my mom crying...trying to hide her pain from my sisters and myself. The midnight hour for a while became a place of healing for my mom. I began to notice that my two older sisters seemed to be impacted by the divorce in a way that mirrored growing pain, or adolescents kicking up in high gear. It was the start of dating in our home, with no real positive male figures to guide them along. We never really talked about our stepdad leaving, I just remember all of us sitting down at the dinner table and he told us he was leaving...there were tears and a lot of misunderstanding floating around that day. We never dealt with it, let along talked about how things changed around us. In our household, there wasn't any real skill set to talk through situations or events...you just moved forward the best you could.

My oldest sister started dating a childhood friend that resulted in a volatile relationship that ultimately left her a single parent with three children to raise. She had great motherly instinct, despite the fact of her having her first daughter when she was only 16 years old.

My middle sister followed suite and became a teenage mother at the age of 16 years old, who also became a single parent to three children. I remember feeling upset when she became pregnant, not really sure why; it could have been the fact of her being closer to my age and attending the same high school when it happened...can't say now; but I believe that if I ponder long enough, I can try to remember why I was upset.

It turns out that I too became a mother at the tender age of 16 years old; at the time I went into internal isolation trying to get through this point in my life, it was very difficult however I got through it with the support of my family. I was in the 11th grade, and I truly didn't understand reproduction and intimacy; I seriously thought that women only became pregnant when they want children, and not a result of anything else...no one ever talked about the "Birds and the

Bee's" with me at home. I remember in sixth grade we had a session on Sex Education that was supposed to reinforce what children were taught at home, unfortunately many households where I grew up never had such discussions, which plagued my community on a large scale. For me, becoming a mother gave me a greater inspiration to do better in life.

I never fully understood the disparities of growing up in a world that looked from the lack point of view, until recently. I always wanted to finish high school, and I did; on time with my graduating class of 1989. There was never a thought that I wouldn't complete high school, despite having a child. I always exceled in school and found learning to be very enjoyable. I had to pick up classes at night school, due to my son being born in spring, and when I returned to school it was near the end of the school year and the classes during the day didn't have space. I managed with the help of my two sisters and my mom. What I was able to complete was definitely because my family supported me and assisted me with taking care of my son. That time of my life was strange, in that; I never thought that would be how my life would be, however I did what I had to do without blaming others for my choices. If I never became a teenage mother, I know for a fact that I would not have had any children at all, it turns out that my son is my one and only child. I love him and having him has made me a stronger woman, driven to keep pushing past setbacks. I had my son during a time where you were put to a public shame at church, thankfully I wasn't brought in front of our congregation to announce my indiscretions. I personally know several friends who lived through the trauma of being on display this way, and I felt the guilt and shame right along with them. I never understood how a community that promotes, or should promote the love of a Savior, could abandon someone broken in this manner. I will never understand that, however I have made a point in being a supportive person that tries to help others get passed barriers without judgement. There are multiple reasons why a person is faced with the issues of life coming at them hard and strong; the last thing a person needs is to be rejected and outcast during a time of need. As a result of this experience, I have worked with youth groups. I know what it is like to be young and in need of assistance from someone that really wants to help.

When the collapse of our family unit resulted in premature motherhood, all of us managed to do the best we could with what we had. My family and I stuck together, and we helped out one another. We did not have many resources, and the struggle was evident throughout the process, however we have endured many obstacles and yet we remained fighters. I can't pretend that life was easy, because it wasn't, nor can I relate a story filled with a false sense of security; but I have come to terms with every aspect of my path, and I look back in humility and not defeat. It's a wonder how I can reflect with a smile on my face, determined not to be overwhelmed with life.

That's my choice, and I exercise the right to take ownership of a healthy recovery.

One observation I have noted about this season of my life, everyone in my environment experienced similar circumstances, that is why I believe it wasn't as devastating. I knew that I wanted to make better choices and provide options for my son that I never had; even if it was just trying to instill in him a drive to overcome real life scenarios without being victimized by life.

I had no positive male figures in my life and come from a history of this in my community. Now I am faced with raising a male child, I made it a point never to bash his father nor any other male. I believe in building people up, and never destroying anyone. I know that we all have had some sort of disadvantage presented in our lives and I will never become a source that perpetuates this vicious cycle. This principle has been the foundation of what I have passed onto my son, and I live by this; and stand on it.

I never wanted to believe the lie of what the world has suggested to me; that I had to be this angry woman. I have no hate in my heart. What I do have is fuel to make a difference. I decided to change the way I viewed life, and in turn move in forward progression. It takes energy to live out a positive way of thinking, and I would not set myself up for failure by wasting time on things that are out of my control. I focus on what I can do, and work towards making that apart of how I get around the pitfalls in life. Perhaps growing up going to church has pointed me to believing in God and using His principles, because it works. My faith in God has always been the best thing going for myself, and it will always be what allows me to keep marching forward.

The absence of a parent in a home has lasting effects on a person, I have witness and experienced emotions that I have seen repeated in many households. I'm uncertain which is the lessor of two evils: A broken two parent home; or the sting of an absent parent...they both can kill the spirit, and make for a life of sorting through unimaginable internal, and emotional issues, if left unattended. How can you deal with abandonment, if you don't know the name of it? Or how can you spot a spotted cow, if you don't know what a cow is; for many they may never know, yet for me; I now know and can seek resolve.

My household was turned upside down, and we knew it; yet there wasn't help. No means of coping with our new set of circumstances, no clear site of what to do. Imagine broken lives, subjected to another generation of lack, absent fathers, poverty, and no resourcefulness. I laugh now as I reflect; but the reality is, none of us had the luxury of giving up nor complaining. Many years have passed, and I can express my thoughts on this time frame of my life, I understand more, and it appears to me that my takeaway is this: I will never feel defeated by the events of life. I have a greater respect for hardship, I choose to remain a fighter. I'm grateful that the devasting life I witnessed, hasn't overtaken me. The reason I can continue is due to me still being alive, which I have determined is enough for me. Do I become hard and callused, no. I desire to be healthy, and for that reason...I stay positive. I don't believe my family has ever talked about what we have endured, I'm sure we all have come to live with the experience, on some level or another, for me I can't share my story without pointing out that these events played a major role in my life. When our stepdad left, our two-parent home was never the same. I don't remember having any tears and didn't even have any questions. I went on as if nothing happened, as everyone else. There was a difference that was felt, even though there was no discussion...now I can clearly point out things that happened that are directly connected to the absence of a father figure. I was unaware at the time of the event; I often think about what may have happened if we had the tools during the event to address what happen...I don't explore that train of thought for long, it won't change what happened, but my reaction to the events has definitely guided me toward dealing with it head on. It was enough to include it in my story, so obviously it hit hard in my life. There had to be forgiveness given to my mom and stepdad for their ignorance on how hurtful their breakup was to myself and my sisters, I look back and understand that now, however at that time there was no clue to what was needed. Perhaps I was able to offer forgiveness, due to being the youngest and possibly the one who totally embraced what we were taught growing up. My sisters I'm sure dealt with this differently than I did, however all of us can and have concluded, that we are able to speak to our stepdad peacefully. It wasn't until I was in my mid- forties that my stepdad had a conversation with me about his departure out of my life, he asked for forgiveness, and I willingly expressed that I didn't hold any hard feelings toward him nor my mom. It was a conversation I'm thankful he had with me, it allowed me to see that he too realized the damaged it caused all of us. And that is how you take what has the potential to destroy and use it for good!

CHAPTER 3

SON, SON, SUNNY

I attended Marston Junior High school, where I was bused from my neighborhood to a predominantly white area; it was 1983 I was crazy about Michael Jackson; break dancing, hip hop and being a valley girl! It was during this time when we had cooking, sewing, and computer classes, most of which are not offered in school now; that's another story. Any who, President Regan was in his first term, and Reaganomics was well underway. Everyone that lived in San Diego in my part of town experienced not having enough of anything simultaneously, and I could see it. I remember earning many awards in my physical education (gym) class, while having holes in my shoes. I had just placed first in a relay race, and my gym teacher took a pollard picture of myself and the two other young ladies that took second and third; I still have the picture, and I remember that day so clear because I stood with my feet angled where the camera wouldn't reveal my poverty. I smile about my lack, but there was nothing cool about wearing Safeway tennis shoes with a hole on the side of them! One of my classmates had a problem going to stores and taking items that didn't belong to her, and she stole several pair of tennis shoes and gave me a pair; which I wasn't with her when she stole them, however I did know how she acquired them; but my need for shoes was greater than my moral convection of receiving stolen goods. One of my other friends also received a stolen pair of snickers, but when she got home her mom discovered them and reported the whole story to the administrators at our school; which ended my acceptance of anything else, but no one knew about the ones I kept. I kept my mouth closed about the details, and my mom never asked me any questions about my new shoes; I do remember saying that my friend at school gave them to me though.

I began my entrance into puberty, and all the hormonal changes that came with it. There was this young man that was two years older than I, who took a liking to me that I began talking to over the phone. He was in my middle sister's class, and he was new to the area, his mother had recently moved from Baltimore Maryland to San Diego. He was the life of any party, he was a jock (he played basketball, and football), and all the girls were crazy over him. I was left to my own devices often during this time of my life (remember my household was upside down from divorce). He and I spent many hours on the phone, falling asleep even many times; and we hung together in our neighborhood as well. We began exploring a sexual relationship when I was 14 years old. I knew nothing, didn't understand nothing; and we were doing what I learned from being around my middle sister as, "what you did," when you have a boyfriend. My middle sister probably wasn't aware that I came to that conclusion as a result of observing the behavior of the older kids I found myself to be with as a default of my sister having to drag me with her where she went. No sad stories, nor blame toward my middle sister; I'm stating facts of my immature, lack of understanding coming of age experience. I believe that everything happens for a reason, and I have no regrets about my life. I can take it all, and hopefully help someone to go in a different direction than what I did, in a hope for a way of providing clear examples of why it's best not to enter into situations that are above certain maturity levels.

I had a friend whose father was a doctor, and she would offer contraceptives to all of us during our gym class; I was so green, that I didn't understand what she was offering nor what it was used for. As a result, I was too embarrassed to ask questions nor accept what she was giving out. I just sat there emotionless, trying to process what transpired. I didn't get it, so I dismissed the whole conversation. I remember my first sexual encounter with this new guy from Baltimore, the thought of, "I don't see the big ideal," that the older girls gossiped about, running across my thoughts...that is what will happen when something is out of order in your life. One thing that happened, was I enjoyed the attention that he gave me, and the companionship we established with one another. He spent time with me, and I felt important and beautiful. Now I can see why it is important for a young lady to have a positive male figure in her life to aid her with having a need to feel loved (the right way), by her father. When your father teaches you how to accept love from a male, you won't have a void in that area; therefore, in my opinion, when you enter into a relationship with a man you will have a clear understanding of what you should engage in and what you shouldn't. This is what I have concluded based upon seeing healthy father daughter relationships. That is one element I wanted to experience with my father, however I didn't receive that. I found myself coming of age, the best I could. I learned mostly by trial and error. Eventually I ended up pregnant at the age of 16 years old by my first love. Now, I grew up during a time when abortions were used as a form of birth control, it was pushed in the media, my environment and the community. I felt the pressure to abort my child all around me. It was readily accessible to me; however, I am thankful that I didn't go that route. I hide my pregnancy, as a result; I didn't receive prenatal care until I was close to 8 months along. In my limited thinking, I was trying to deal with the issue on my own, I felt like it was my business...silly me, I didn't have any business! I never understood nor considered how we would take care of the baby. I had no clue where money would come from; and honestly none of that entered my thoughts. All I knew was he loved me and I him and that was more than enough for me. He was my first, and he was such a giver; I never had thoughts of not having what was needed; rather financially or emotionally. I wasn't concerned about any of those things, I didn't know I should have been. I watched people around me do what they had to do for their children, and I didn't think that I would do anything less than that. When my family discovered that I was having a baby, I'm sure they took it hard; matter of fact I know they did. I remember being in quiet mode during my whole pregnancy. I was in 11th grade by now; and to make the transition into motherhood easy on me, I transferred to Crawford High School, in San Diego, California. One of my dearest friends that I went to junior high with, transferred there and I decided that it would be a good change of environment for me; manly so I could deal with the shame and guilt I had about being pregnant as a teenager. I figured that I wouldn't have such a hard time dealing with my peers at school and all the whispers, and stares that would come my way. Mind you, I and my family went through this together; while attending a black church. Now, for those of you that don't know; having a child out of wedlock; while being a minor and poor; whose mother was a single parent...that had two older daughters that just went through the same experience...wasn't good. You talking about being shunned, outcast, and the topic of many gossip sessions, that was what occurred in my life. So, there I was, dealing with all these heavy circumstances, at the ripe age of 16 years old. I know for a fact that many others experienced this same narrative, it was common and sad. I'm glad I was able to get through this difficult part of my history. I gave birth to a healthy baby boy; my son was what I needed, and God knew it. I was a single parent that had the support of my immediate family, as a result of this support system I was able to manage this new stage of my life. Looking back, there were real hard points within this journey; my goodness I'm excited that I can say that with a chuckle and a smile!

The Other Side of Healing

My son's father and I were kids, and I chalk up the entire time frame as being a situation surround by immaturity, as a bottom line; he and I broke up and he moved back to Baltimore. My son has always known who his father is and where his father was, and now that time and life has moved on; the two of them have a wonderful relationship. His father loves him, and he loves his dad.

There were many times during my son's upbringing, where I had to cover for the absence of his father, my son felt the pain that so many know so well; that being the longing for the connection and bonding of a father and son. There were many lessons my son had to learn, the best way he could, as a woman I have often said that I couldn't teach him things that only a father can teach a son. I gave what I had, and I raised my son the best I could with what I had. My love toward him allowed me to be a source of encouragement for him, and often he served as the catalyst that made me fight barriers and setbacks harder than what I knew I had in me to fight. It's amazing how while your smack dab in the midst of a situation, you don't fully understand the dynamics; that's one variable in an equation that never adds up at times. My son, son, sunny will always be the sunshine that pointed to a brighter day for me, without a second thought I know this to be a truth for me.

CHAPTER 4

DR. DEAN

It's a typical Friday night in San Diego, CA in 1990; my two older sisters and two of our friends and myself are headed towards Coronado base to be entertained for the evening. At this point in my life my son was two years old, I just celebrated my 19th birthday; New Jack Swing music was cranking on 92.5 FM radio dial, I was enrolled in Paralegal school, and I was well on my way to what was next in my life. I absolutely loved the language of the law; I had found what I wanted to do with my life! I was going to school, and everything seemed to be working well for me. I was two weeks away from the completion of the paralegal course, I was top in my class and looking forward to what was next. One day leading to the last week of the program, one of the administrators of the school came into my class and inform us that our instructor had quit, and she took all of our grades, and assignments; and refused to turn them over to the school so we could graduate. We were devastated, what would become of all of the assignments that we completed so we could receive our certificates of completion? We all had so many questions and no one had answers for us. I was upset, frustrated, and felt like I was defrauded. Two days later, the school informed my class that the only way they would give us our certificates for the course, was for us to redo the whole program. This was a nine-month course of hard work doing legal documents and research; I was against the very thought of doing it all over again. I decided not to repeat the program, and I walked away from the paralegal world. I was disgusted. This was also a time where I found myself hanging out going to parties, and enjoying the balance of motherhood, school and coming of age!

All of us met up at my house, my older sister and her three children were back living with my mom, my son, and I. We lived off Home Avenue, near Hollywood Park. My older middle sister lived with her husband and her children near Chula Vista. One of our friends was dating one of the most popular Disc Jockeys in San Diego, the other friend was closer to my middle sister, and we were all planning to enjoy the evening out sharing some girl time together. Often you would find us hanging out with our friends and enjoying every minute of our time together! Tonight, was no different. We all jumped into the white Ford Escort that my friend drove, and off we went. If you have never been to San Diego, let me share some information with you. The weather is absolutely one of the main reasons people pay so much to reside in California, they have the best Mexican food you can imagine, and you can exercise outdoors pretty much all year long! We took the beautiful drive over the Coronado bridge to get to the Amphibious base. We parked outside and walked through the gate of the base, to the building where the event was being held. I recall the details of this night for many reasons; as we walked into the venue, there was this odd ball feeling that overtook me. I instantly felt out of place, and as though all eyes were staring at us. I have never felt like I didn't belong in any setting I have been in, so to have this immediate thought from entering a place where we were the only black faces...was unsettling. Please understand, I'm from a city in California that has a very diverse demographic of residents, and I have grown up with white people all my life! At this point I had experienced more racism within the black community, with the whole light skin, dark skin nonsense; than I had with direct racism coming from someone white. To have this sudden feeling of not belonging, was weird to say the least. As a result of my internal thoughts guiding my actions, I felt the need to do something to make me relax a bit, so I could enjoy the girl's night out. We had come to be entertained by being in the audience of a hypnotist. First off, my sister's and I was reared in a God fearing home where, we were taught that this kind of activity was of the devil.... looking back, I really didn't understand what that really meant. I did the unimaginable, I raised my hand and volunteered to be hypnotized along with my good friend that came to the show also. I was thinking that this participation would help me chill out, oh my, was I wrong.

The auditorium was large, there wasn't a vacate seat in the place. The lighting was dark, and the host of the event gave all of us that volunteered a seat on the platform where he began to hypnotize us. The host went by the stage name of, "Dr. Dean" and before I knew it; I was a character preforming on stage! I don't really remember all, of what Dr. Dean had us doing, but I do remember that it felt like I had no control over what I was doing. The best way for me to describe what was going on is to say this, the things I had no control over was put in front of my mind, and the things that I could control was placed in the back of my mind. I was aware, but unaware, in a fog or stupor. I was in a dream like state of being, doing things that were suggested to me by the host. It was all a part of the entertainment for the night, and I didn't understand how this church going young lady, such as myself could even be in this scene, but there I was. If only I had known, I was taught better, however I didn't understand the why of how I even volunteered for such a thing! I'm no psychologist, therapist, nor behavior specialist; and at the time of this night in my life, I had no point of reference for any of the events that occurred to me, and I will attempt to share my experience from my point of view to the best of my ability.

Allow me to explain how I understand what happened to me, using a basic explanation. The show went on, and when it was time for the entertainment to conclude for the evening, the host went through the process of bringing the volunteers from under his hypnotic trance. He began to count from 100 to 1. I remember my concentration being broke somewhere during the process, when this happened, I distinctively recall feeling like, uh oh, something doesn't feel right. I could tell that something was way off center, however I did not express to anyone that I felt this way.

We left and went home. I was restless the whole night, and I couldn't sleep. I tossed and turned all night. I continued to go about my daily routine, with taking care of my son. It was a regular day in my world, except for feeling drained from getting no sleep. I didn't know to think much of my inability to sleep that first night. Then the next night was about the same, no sleep and extremely restless. I can say now that my concentration was off, and my thoughts were working overtime in my mind. I could not stop my thoughts from racing, it was like a leaking faucet that drips continuously with no valve to turn off the main water line. The lack of sleep continued, and my behavior became unlike me. I was answering people that talked to me off what they were thinking and not from what they were saying to me. I was acutely aware of every little thing around me, I could see and hear on a level; that no one else could see nor hear. There were times during this ordeal that it felt as though my spirit had left my body and I could see and hear people from other dimensions and locations.

My family noticed the difference in my behavior, and they knew something was wrong with me, but this was 1990 and my family had no idea what was going on with me. What my family knew was I didn't drink, smoke or use drugs. I wasn't on any medication; I was a vivacious healthy 19-year-old young lady with my whole life in front of me.

My mom decided that she would take me back up to the Amphibious base to see Dr. Dean and find out what he did to me and what could he do to help me. When we arrived at the base my mom met with Dr. Dean and explained that I wasn't sleeping, and I was acting strange. He began to explain to my mom that he was legally blind and could only see shadows, and he tried to put me back under hypnoses, and when that didn't work; he told my mom that there wasn't anything he could do for me. We left and I'm sure my mom had many thoughts of sorrow and disappointment as we drove back home.

At the time I weighed 125 pounds at 5 feet 9 inches tall, I wasn't sleeping nor was I eating properly. I was hearing voices, and delusional. I was extremely confused and disoriented. During this time my overall health was rapidly declining, and no one had a clue what was happening to me.

My family attended Israelite Church of God in Christ and the church had just relocated to the big building on 43rd street off Imperial Avenue, near the Educational Cultural Complex (ECC). I want to be clear on what I am saying, and how I convey the details…I want to go on record to say that I have no ill feelings toward my church, nor my church family at that time. I want to point out how people in the church world handled my unique situation, without proper training. They handled it the best they knew how with what they had. In no means am I suggesting that what occurred was right, but I do not hold anyone at fault. Various members of the church had gotten word that I was, get this "demon possessed," and several people decided to come by our home during the time I was displaying erratic behavior to help cast out the demons and or pray for me. Remember, this is 1990, and my family attended a predominantly black church that demonized everything due to being undereducated and severely misinformed about my condition. One thing for sure, the church and the members believed in the power of prayer. When a few of the members of the church came by our house, they witnessed firsthand my condition at its worse. They didn't know what to do, so they prayed and left, then gossiped about what they thought was going on with me. No one had any experience with anything that resemble what I was going through, so it is unrealistic for me to be angry or bitter about their treatment of me. My immediate family members were at a total disadvantage as well.

My family watched as I faded into this state of being that was dark, and very scary. I was totally unlike the me that they knew and loved. There is nothing sadder than to stand by and be defenseless against an attack on one of your loved ones. You can't help in any tangle way that makes the person go back to who they are, so what do you do? You don't know who to call for help, you can't explain what is happening, all that can be done; my family was doing it...which was to pray. My mom has always been a powerful woman of God, hands down; even she was looking for some relief for her child. I was being tormented right before their very eyes.

One day during this ordeal my grandma Dolly suggested that my mom take me to see some Mexican spiritual women, in hopes of this woman pulling me out of this altered state of mind. My mom was so loving in her desperate attempt to help me that she found herself and my grandma loading me into the car and driving to this lady's house. As we pulled up to the house, my mom recalls the spirit of the Lord Jesus, speaking to her, telling her that I would be worse off if she took me to see this spiritualist. My mom came to herself and probably made the best decision she could, and they drove off without even touching the sidewalk of that home. Looking back now, and fully understanding the gravity of what could have happened to me is frightening. I'm so thankful that my mom drove off.

This out of control, unknown, unnamed event went on like this for about 2 weeks before my family sought medical help for me. I was running out of the house without clothes on, I was on my menstrual cycle and wouldn't keep my sanitary napkin on...I was in a bad way and something had to be done about it. My mom came into my room and tried to get me to put my clothes and personal items back on, to no avail. I became violent and struck my mom, my mom spoke to the strong demonic force that was trying to overtake my mind and body. She declared that the devil could not have my mind. I had become harmful to myself and everyone around me. My oldest sister was so scared, she went into her room with her three children and my son and barricaded the door and pleaded with my mom to call the police for help.

Tichamingo White

One of my godbrothers came into the room where I was, to get me to put my clothes on; in an effort of lending his support; and I began to attack him viciously. It was at this point the authorities were called. When the authorities arrived, one police officer assessed the situation, once my mom explained what occurred, the officer asked if I were on drugs and wanted to know if my mom wanted to press charges on me for my violent outburst. My mom was totally offended at his approach to the situation, and matter-of-factly stated that I wasn't on drugs, and this wasn't me and let him know that pressing charges on me wasn't going to help the situation at all. She wasn't sure what was going on, she just wanted them to get me some help. There were two police officers, two EMS workers, my mom and my godbrother that tried to get me on the gurney and strap me in. I broke free the first time out of the restraints when only the EMS workers tried to tie me down, it wasn't until everyone on the scene worked together, that they were able to get me into the ambulance and transport me to Grossmont Hospital.

CHAPTER 5

LOCKED UNIT

A s I was rushed to the behavior health department of Grossmont Hospital, there was an officer that was assigned to keep watch over me, while I was admitted into the hospital. While waiting for the doctors to determine what to do for me, I remember feeling drained, and out of it. I was disconnected from myself and didn't know it. The two weeks that my health declined, I had no ability to help myself nor express that I was in a crisis mode and needed assistance. That is one component of my experience that I will never fully be able to describe, the inability of saying, HELP ME!

One could never come to terms with being in a state of mind where you can't think clearly to go about living your regular life. Many of the details of my experience I personally remember, and few of the events I don't remember; perhaps this is the way the brain protects one from trauma. For example, I have no recall of striking my mom; I do recall the attack on my godbrother. The brain is a powerhouse, designed to preserve, protect, and heal itself. The analogy I have come to embrace, as a means of understanding, and explaining what took place in my brain is this: The brain is like a computer; if there is an overload of info, the computer will shut down in an attempt to protect what is stored in the computer. My brain experienced a major overload that it could not handle, so it had to shut down and reboot.

It was a very painful process, slipping from reality into a foggy supernatural realm that isn't meant for anyone to exist in. This was and has been my thoughts for many reasons. As the years have come and gone since this saga of my life, I have come to learn and understand more about my unique experience.

There I was, in the hospital in the behavior health unit. At the time, I had never heard the term, let alone knew what it meant. What I knew was this intrusive event rendered me in what I thought to be a helpless situation.

I was admitted into the hospital initially in the open unit where I had the liberty of not being confined nor restricted to the point of requiring being monitored close. Being in the open unit didn't last long, my condition had me unable to make decisions that kept me and others around me safe. I had to be cared for in a manner that prevented me from self-harm. Remember I had no control over what I was doing, and no memory of most of the bizarre actions.

The doctors decided that I needed medication to help my brain slow down and bring me into a manageable state of being. Most of what I am expressing from the medical perspective was told to me way after the fact, I was in a cave in my mind, and I didn't know how I got there nor how I got out. All I remember was that it was a place off the grid, oblivion an abyss of all the negative descriptive words you can name; even still coming up with no formulation of words to depict what I endured.

I remember zoning in and out of myself, giving me a few minutes of me and more time spent in this vegetable like shell of me; that I didn't recognize. During the events, it was as if I was the main character in a sad devastating debilitating eerie movie, that had a plot that sucked you into the story and held you captive. It played out to the fullest in the most mundane backdrop. An unimaginable twist of events that could not be explained. However, the key characters didn't want to be a star in the movie, nor be featured in this chilling thriller. Unwilling participants we most certainly were, one would never wish nor foresee such a cruel storyline. That was how I viewed it, and I just wanted to escape the torment and anguish that seemed like there was no start nor end of it. I have come to describe this hospitalization as a day that forever changed the course of my life.

My mom would come to the hospital every day to see me and check on me. One of the doctors told my mom that it wasn't a good idea for her to come see me every day; he probably thought this was good advice, considering the state and nature of my condition. There was a nurse that overheard the doctor give his suggestions, and when she had the chance, she privately pulled my mom to the side and encouraged her to continue to check on me. The nurse stated that my mom had the right to check on her child, and to make sure that I was being cared for properly. It was a good thing my mom came to the hospital every day, because the doctors had me over medicated and my family and friends were grossly saddened to see me out of my head like that.

My mom didn't know if the high dosage of medication was helping or making me worse. If my mom hadn't come up to the hospital daily; she would not have been able to demand that the doctors reduce the medication. Upon the first day in the hospital, I was placed on a 72-hour hold. This in simple terms; is when someone involuntarily is detained when they have an emergency mental condition that allows treatment and psychiatric evaluation. The doctors scrambled to determine what was best and they carried it out.

At some point during the back and forth with my care and family and friends coming to visit me; the doctors, social workers, and the care team called my immediate family into a meeting to explain what happened, and what their diagnosis, and prognosis was. These accounts were shared with me later; the main doctor explained to my family that I had a psychotic break, which meant that I had left reality and was in an unreal state of existence. The doctor further determined that I would never regain my sanity nor be able to care for my son or myself any longer; and that I would always need someone to care for me.

I can't imagine how my family felt once they heard this information, I know that this information was very disturbing, and it cut my family deeply and greatly impacted our family bound like never before.

Tichamingo White

When life drives a nail into the routine of daily occurrences, it will leave you on four flat tires without any tools or resources to help you figure out the next move. This event had the potential of resetting the direction of not only my life, but all that were connected to me.

How could this be happening, you may be wondering; the answer is simple, it occurs more frequently than I ever knew at the time. Situations look different when they happen to you, I believe tragedy has a way of forcing you to realize that life is short. I know that all the events that happened to me and my family, proved to be mile markers that showcased the true strength we possessed.

When loved ones and friends wanted to come check on me while I was in the critical stage of my hospitalization; my mom would try to coach them and prepare them for what they would see when they entered my hospital room. She thought it best to encourage them to maintain their composure in front of me... but how do you expect loved ones to respond to seeing someone so young and full of life, whom you seen a few weeks ago and was, "normal" in this unfamiliar state of being? My mom didn't want anyone to break down in front of me once they seen me in that altered state of mind. I was very sensitive to the people I came in contact with, and my mom wasn't certain how I would react to family and friends coming apart emotionally. Many of them couldn't keep it together, it was down rite heart breaking. My mom told me after I got better, that my stepfather, (the one I grew up with); broke down in tears when he came up to the hospital to see me. Whenever someone is faced with a life altering circumstance, that no one can fix...what is one to do? It will tear your heart out of your chest and cause you to reach a very sad place that no doctor can mend. Think about, your loved one sick, and you can't make it go away. I had to go through this, my family went also. At the time my situation felt like slow death, or better put, torment. The mental agony played out long and slow, a continuous drip that gets louder by the minute. Think of the worse physical pain you have ever experienced, now intensify that, and add no sleep, extreme muscle fatigue, and internal noise that wouldn't turn off. These symptoms also came with delusions, visions, and vivid dreams. I didn't know if I were coming or going, or perhaps both.

I found myself while being in the locked unit, running into other patient's rooms; without any knowledge or thought of being there. I would hide behind curtains that had cobwebs and dust particles, when the staff would find me, my face and hair would tell on me. They told me not to wonder off into other people's rooms, but of course I was driven with a force that had control over me, and I was taken on a journey, not only physically, but mentally as well. If I had not lived through this event myself, I would probably have a hard time believing a story like mine.

The locked unit housed people from all walks of life. Some of the people were stuck in certain time periods and couldn't get out. I remember one lady that thought she was living in the 1960's, her clothes reflected the pictures I had seen from old movies from that era. She had on stripped bellbottoms, a shirt with a flower and glasses with pointed frames. I remember her because she was very nice to me, which made it hard to understand why she tried to slice her wrist. One of the male patients had to be checked on every 10 minutes and couldn't be left alone, he had tried to castrate himself. Most of the patients would walk back and forth, pacing the small narrow hallway of the locked unit talking to themselves, just sad, sad, and downright depressing. On one occasion I went on the patio on the locked unit, these were the days people could smoke outdoors on the hospital grounds; I was holding a conversation internally with God, but verbally talking out loud. There was this older white lady, that came over to me and started holding my hand and telling me how connected to the universe I was, she also told me that God was with me. I mentioned this because one thing I was completely aware of, was the fact that God was real, and so was the adversary. These were some of the patients that I shared the locked unit with. If you were in the locked unit, you were bad off. I remember that my condition was so severe that they had to put me in the isolation room. I have a vague memory of there being a stained-glass window in the room and I was out to lunch, my cheese had slid off of the cracker, my thoughts and imagination had left me and went into some unknown location. I write this today with a chuckle and a smile of thankfulness that I can make light of my condition, I'm not trying to be insensitive to anyone who is currently going through something similar...I'm just telling my story.

That's one thing no one can take nor steal, my narrative. I tell my story how it went for me; God has allowed me to see the beauty of the experience. I retell the events surrounding the ordeal with joy and not disparity. Each time I share what occurred to me, it gives me strength, hope, and victory. Strength to continue fighting for Mental Health Advocacy. Hope that my story will help others. Victory in knowing that I'm not defeated by what transpired. This is actually the first time I am sharing my story without reservations. When I have shared my story in times past, I would only give bits and pieces. I would determine how much I would share, depending on what I decerned the hearing could handle. One thing I know for sure, is many people can't handle the weight of a story line that is laced with an unknown area. Usually, when the scope of subject hasn't been known to the hearer, it is very difficult to wrap your brain around the concepts. Nonetheless I'm eager to give all of the points to my story, it's time.

While in the locked unit, the staff try to engage the patients in group theory sessions. These sessions are designed to help the patients reconnect with the real world and others in it. When I was in the critical state, I wasn't aware of myself nor others. I imagine that the sessions are really for the staff to determine how bad off someone is, in an attempt to report to the doctors. This allows for the doctors to decide on what approach they would take to help the patients. The more group sessions you attended and participated in throughout the course of the day, signified that your condition was getting better. I recall making an effort to participate in the group sessions, this was after the medication was balanced in my system and I wasn't moving like a robot any longer. I didn't want to be in the hospital no longer than I had to be there. Once I realized that I was in the hospital, I wanted to go home with my family and would cry when I couldn't leave with them when they came to see me. That is a bad feeling, wanting to go home and you can't. The freedom to decide what to do, when you want to do it, is precious. When you can't make sound decisions for yourself, it robes you of feeling in control of your life. I felt sad, and desponded, a very low dark place. Something deep on the inside of me felt shattered, broken, and empty. During my forced stay in the locked unit, I often found myself praying and crying out to God. I knew that He would be my only help out of this situation. There were times that to the naked eye, I appeared to be staring off in the distance but not looking at anything in particular, what is defined as a catatonic state of being. During these times, my spirit was communing with God. I was in the presence of God. It felt safe, warm, and free: Safe from the torment of not being able to turn my thoughts off; warm, which also felt like assurance, and free from the grip of death; a holding pattern of sorts. I wasn't sure of where I was nor any thought that I needed to be concerned with why I was there either. As time passed, not necessarily a space of time; more like the strength of life reentering my body; I became aware that where my spirit was, wasn't designed for me to stay there for an extended period of time. Everything I knew, or thought I knew from a biblical spiritual standpoint suggested that this was a spiritual location, and the exact destination was unknown and extremely unfamiliar to me. I heard talk as a child about spiritual experiences that fit the criteria of this place that I somehow had entered into, however I never heard any description given of torment or pain when entering this place. I'm uncertain if the pain, agony, and torment was caused by what occurred to me at the hands of the hypnotist; the opening up of portholes in my mind that rendered me subjected to both the bad and good elements of the spiritual realm; or was it the penalty of disobedience of engaging in a satanic practice that opened the door into the spiritual realm? I understand that from childhood God had given me a keen awareness and sensitivity to the spiritual realm, and what took place when I went to the hypnotist show altered the natural gifting that God gave me; my natural ability to filter how I processed the spiritual realm went into overload, where the speed of incoming info was overwhelming. My thoughts ran at an accelerated pace that would not turn off nor stop, which caused sleep deprivation. The lack of sleep caused the visions and dreams that I normally was able to handle to be in high throttle to the point of confusion. Everything was taken out of its natural rhythm and was tossed into a chaotic mumble jumbo that could not be deciphered. I was locked up, in a state that had a tight hold on me. Held captive, a prisoner in the bonds of the unknown. I call it unknown, however God knew where I was, and He also was with me while there. You may find that hard to believe, everything that you have been taught about God never told you that

46

despite how I got to the where of where I was; yet instill God had His hand on me and He most certainly was with me. How can I say that with surety? Had God not been with me, I would have forever lost my mind then, with no possibility to retell my story or regain my sanity. My experience speaks to God's plan for my life and not my own, I understand that what happen to me was a mere encounter that set me up to be God's witness. I must point others in God's direction, for He and Him alone is the only hope someone may have of finding rest from Mental anguish and torment. I now understand how a situation meant to destroy me, has opened up an opportunity to reach back and pull someone else out of the disparity of the complications of Mental crisis.

I remember at one-point while being in the locked unit that my behavior was out of control to the point of me running while no one was chasing me. This put the staff in a difficult situation, I'm sure due to the potential of me harming myself or someone else. The staff had me tied in a chair, I tried to toss and turn to get out of the restraints. I was unable to break free, my efforts left me to black out and go into a protective place in my mind. I came to, and one of the staff members was making faces and making fun of me. When you are in the hospital out of your mind, you are at the mercy of the staff, you never know what these people are doing to you. All you have to protect you is God. I remember one of my doctors lost his license due to sexual misconduct and gross negligence in 1994, I wasn't one of the patients that he abused but I share this information in an attempt of discussing the dark components of treatment that no one talks about. This is also why family members should randomly check on their loved ones in the hospital.

I'm grateful that my family was able to get help for me, so many people in the black community don't know about Mental Health resources and it is time to become aware of what to do if you or someone you come in contact with is in need of professional assistance. There are many treatment methods, and no two people will respond the same way to the care that is available. The most important thing is to know that it is okay to get help for a Mental condition, often people suffer alone, and you shouldn't feel afraid nor ashamed for caring for yourself. I will go into further details about how I sought help and what helped me at another time.

CHAPTER 6

NUT JOB

I was in the hospital for almost three weeks before I came back to more of me, and less of what happened to me. Mind you the doctors told my family that I would never be in my right state of mind again. I was released from Grossmont Hospital with a prescription for Haldol and Cogentin. Haloperidol is used to rebalance dopamine (something your body makes, that your nervous system uses to send messages between nerve cells. It has a big impact on how you plan, think and feel pleasure) and to improve thinking, mood, and behavior. Cogentin is used to counter act the involuntary muscle movements that some people experience when taking an antipsychotic medication. I had an appointment to follow up with my new doctor that specialized in treating patients that have mental disturbances as well. I don't recall any medical providers explaining to me what happened, nor do I remember any real education on how to proceed once I left for home. It was as if someone said, "*take two of these, and call me in the morning!*"

When I came home, my motor skills were off. I was moving slow and everything around me appeared to be new. The sound of birds in the trees seemed to be louder than I would have preferred to hear at that time. My eyes had a crisp colorful intake as I admired the beauty of the radiant flowers that were in bloom, and I could smell the musk on a mouse ten miles away.   Sensory overload is what I now know it to be, at the time I felt as if it were my first time being outdoors ever; except with a point of reference for what my brain had a recall of. I had never known that the body, and brain could calibrate to the point of ingesting my surroundings with such clarity. It was awkward, and I felt the nervousness and fear from my loved ones of their concern of, "is she really okay," and I could sense that they were uncertain if I would get sick all over again. We all were eager to move past what occurred, but not sure of how to deal with me being home after such a traumatizing event. I'm sure my family was tired and many of them probably just needed a good night of rest, we all were drained even though no one made mention of their feelings. I felt glad to be home even though I was numb and void of expressions. My son was two years old, and I remember needing my families support with his care. My mom and sisters all pitched in and rallied around me in whatever capacity they could. It meant a lot to me, having them there with me...I'm thankful for a strong support system.

In the days that followed, I was taking it easy. My mom tried to filter who came by to see me and encouraged me to just stay calm and get plenty of sleep. I lost about 15 pounds during this whole ordeal, as if I had it to lose, I didn't! My mom and oldest sister made sure I had enough to eat, in hopes of me recovering sooner. I could feel the love from my family, and I know that is what nourished me back to where I needed to be. It was a slow road to recovery, I had no clue what to expect once I got home, but it was just refreshing to be alive.

When I went to my follow up appointment with my new doctor, I wasn't prepared to hear what he had to say to me. I walked into his office, and I sat across from his desk, and he looked at me and said, "I'm glad you're not a flake anymore, when you came to the hospital, you were seeing things, hearing voices and acting bazar, a real nut job!" Those words cut deep, imagine not understanding what happen to me, and no medical professional educating me nor trying to help me process what to do or anything! I wasn't expecting his bedside manner to be so rude, insensitive, and downright inappropriate. I was expecting him to go over what happen and what I needed to do or some sort of guidance through the scenario. Instead, I felt insulted, humiliated, and violated. The doctor went on to say that I could stop taking the medication since I was better now and that there was no need for me to come back. I was glad that he dismissed me, and I couldn't get out of his office fast enough! I never shared with anyone exactly what he said to me, I really just wanted to move on. What he said has always stayed with me, for many reasons; he was also the doctor that met with my family in the hospital and wrote me off as never regaining my sanity. I never viewed myself the way the doctor described me as, but I couldn't help but feel beaten down. Instead of him answering the millions of questions floating around in my head that I didn't know how to ask, he added further injury by depicting me as someone that had the option of choosing how I was behaving verses someone who couldn't make heads or tails over the symptoms I displayed. What a total disappointment to the medical community, how dare he handle people in such a disrespectful manner. Looking back this speaks volumes to many of the barriers to proper care that many people experience. It's no wonder many people decide to take matters into their own hands and go without the care of medical doctors. I want to be clear on the fact of me never giving up on me, the way that the medical professionals failed me. I don't blame them; I'm expressing how I felt about my experience. We lived in a world that during this time, 1990; little information and education was given in poor black communities about Mental Health. Honestly until recently, there wasn't much research nor funding allocated towards this social issue.

Even though I had no real understanding of this world of Mental Health, people that I witnessed up to this point, whom may have displayed some sort of Mental condition were never viewed in a functioning part of society. I would hear terms of what people labeled them to be, however I don't recall anyone speaking about how to help these individuals. Often, social issues don't impact you on a personal level until it's you or someone connected to you going through it; that makes it of real concern. This is usually the way advocacy begins, out of the need to help a loved one affected by the debilitating effects of trauma. I guess it is like the saying, "it's not a problem, until it's a problem." Looking back, this was a strange way to be introduced to a social issue that most people have no idea about the long-term effects of.

I witnessed people doing a lot of labeling, and defining people with mental health conditions, in my opinion most of it is due to lack of education, or under education on the subject matter. Also fear of what is not known causes many to try to explain away what they don't understand. Whatever causes a person to arrive at categorizing people in need of professional help, makes me wonder about how cruel this is to the people that are being labeled. Words are damaging, and may cause internal injury, of which many people never heal from.

I decided during this doctor's visit, that I would get far away from this doctor's view of me, even though I didn't know much about the who, what, and why's of my experience, I most certainly wasn't going to subject myself to be in the presence of someone who made me feel worse about what happen to me. This was an open and shut case, the doctor gave me the clearance to go on with my life as I knew it, and I looked forward to getting stronger and resuming my normal lifestyle. In plain English, the doctor released me from his care and took me off the medication cold turkey.

As I recall what happened to me, I also welcomed the thought of not needing to be seen by anymore doctors, no more periods of being lost in space and not understanding what was going on. When the doctor cleared and dismissed me, I cleared and dismissed the whole experience as well...good rittens! I was 19 years old, and I didn't have a clue that what just happen to me was only the beginning. There was no way for me to know that there was a world of people that fell into this new category that I was unintentionally inducted into.

During the first three months after my hospitalization, I noticed that every month around the same time, I would break out with these unsightly black spots around my eyes, arms, and legs. I was uncertain of what those spots were, so I made an appointment to go to the dermatologist. When I went to the doctor, the dermatologist couldn't offer much help, probably due to the fact that the spots had cleared up by the time I had the appointment; so, I went back home. A few weeks went by and the spots reappeared from what seemed to be nowhere, and I couldn't pen point no particular catalyst.

After six months had passed and the spots would go and come, I just accepted them as a part of my life; I didn't know at the time that they were connected to what happen to me when I had the mental health crisis, now I can trace so many things to my body chemistry being out of whack. I don't know if it was the health care system in San Diego or just the care that I received, but none of the providers I seen had any solutions to what I was going through. The dermatologist gave me hydrocortisone cream and that was it. To my surprise looking back, none of the health care specialist made any connections to my mental health for all of the new issues I faced. This doctor didn't refer to that one and vice versa, so my overall care didn't cover much so I began moving forward without being under the care of any doctor. I didn't have any symptoms that directly resembled my behavior while in the hospital for the mental breakdown, so as far as everyone; including myself was concerned I had no need for a physician.

I wasn't the burst of endless internal and external natural glee that I was prior to the mental breakdown. At one point, I laughed a lot and was easy going, and at times; down rite sexy goofy! This new me had a sadness that I can't explain, hollow on the inside and blank. My new expression was so unlike me, I felt the difference...I'm sure those around me could see the drastic difference as well. All of who I knew myself to be prior to this mental intrusion, had checked out and left the room dark. I have never been a dark emotional person, and this gloominess that entered my life was not wanted nor welcomed. If mood were a color, I would describe myself as orange before, and after the event pale grey. It's strange how circumstances, and situations can wipe the natural smile off of a person, leave you in a state of trying to process information with no help. I'm not certain if I did have all the education, resources, and explanations from care providers at that time; if it would have made the new sadness easier to work through. What I now understand, is that I was stripped down from the inside out, my banana was split; and there is no real explanation of how to cope, nor deal with such an unwanted health dilemma. It was definitely an undesirable state of being, to say the least. The scariest part of the whole equation is that, after the first 20 years of trying to revive the old me; I connected the dots and could see that the root issue steamed from the breakdown. All of the times I became withdrawn, closed off, and disconnected from others; I finally could corelate the differences, so it was time to repair, mend, and restore what I lost. I knew that there was a part of me that I enjoyed and loved that had died, as I'm reviewing those two decades; I actually began to work on helping myself and I didn't even realize that was happening. I woke up after 20 years and can say that it was as if it was a sudden turn around, however the road that led me to where I am today was not instantaneous. There were internal effects that manifested outwardly in my life that at the time, I did not understand.

Let me walk down this for you, when I had this break down, I was fresh out of high school, and I was enrolled in my first college courses; eagerly anticipating graduating and gaining sustainable employment. My peers were off to their college experiences as well, the whole world before us. There were times that my concentration was off, and I couldn't make heads or tails of what was occurring to me. I had always earned high achievements in school, so for me not to be able to focus on whatever task I was engaged in, was alarming. I'm going through on the inside, and not expressing it to anyone. I was lost, in an unfamiliar place that didn't make sense to me. I'm restating this to express the importance of what I'm trying to convey, my life, my world had been flipped and It wasn't a matter of hitting a switch and going back to who I was previously. For the joy that I had to be more dominate as before, I had to scramble, bob and weave to ensure that I could see me again and less of the breakdown. There were many times of uncertainty and nights full of tears. All I could do was pray and plead with God to help me find balance. When you have a point of reference from a good place to something other than that, you long for the good. My life after the episode was full of events that centered around being healthier mentally. I found myself looking for internal peace to calm all of the loud noise that was interfering with who I once was. I love myself and I was determined that these feelings, emotions and behaviors couldn't ruin who I was. I set out to turn my situation into a manageable outcome that I could have and not it ruling me. There were days I didn't want to deal with what happened to me. Often, I grew sick of having to find new ways of staying upbeat and positive while having this under current of blues running reckless on the inside of me. I missed me, and I wanted her back. Have you ever been around someone that brightens the air that you are breathing, yeah that is how I feel about who I was. As I go back to the road of yesterday, and see what it took and takes to maintain a well-rounded internal me; it is a constant act of targeting the bull's eye and shooting as close to the center as possible. There are no off days, however it has become an involuntary action in my existence. That doesn't mean that I get to stop aiding myself, it simply means that no one can "clock," my off days. I would never want to mask or suppress what is occurring on the inside of me, I had to learn how to be aware and do something so that I don't lose what I have gained. I have come to the place where my journey from being called a, "nut job," has afforded me the fortitude to speak up and be the voice that many don't have.

CHAPTER 7

OH, YOU AGAIN

I found myself accepting the spots that appeared on my skin, as if they were always a part of me. It's amazing how you can adapt to certain circumstances due to not having any other options available. When I had the spots on my skin, they would leave scars. I tried a few different types of lotion to moisturize the area, in an attempt of not having dry rough skin on top of dealing with the spots. I have come to know that petroleum jelly worked best, so that has been the number one go to that I used on my skin.

I enrolled in one of the local junior colleges in San Diego and I began taking college courses. I wasn't sure what I wanted my degree in, I just knew that I would earn my degree. I noticed that I was still excited about learning, however there was a difference in my ability to handle pressure or demands. I never took noticed to any thoughts associated with being overwhelmed with day -to- day responsibilities, so I continued doing what I had always done. I would plan, set goals and work hard to complete the task. I decided to stop taking college courses, and I decided to try another vocational school to attend, this time I took a dental assistant training because a close friend was in the dental field, and she encouraged me to take the course. Once again, I found myself excelling in yet another program, and I enjoyed what I was doing.

My family was proud of me, everything was going great. I wasn't under a doctor's care, and I wasn't taking any medication. I was living according to what I wanted to do, I was dating and taking care of my son.

The dental assistant course was a nine-month course and I had to complete externship hours before I would receive my certificate of completion; my instructor for my class referred me to a local dentist that she knew, I contacted the dental office and the doctor agreed to allow me to complete my clinical hours at his practice.

I found myself working non-stop. On the last day of my externship, the dentist offered me a permanent position, and I accept the job! It was a great opportunity to earn a living and it felt good being able to provide for myself and my son. The dentist taught me everything from the front office to the back office, at one point I trained other dental assistants that came for their externship as well. The dental office I worked at was on Federal Boulevard and I worked for a black dentist. It was a small private practice, and we were a close nit group. The dentist was like a father figure to his staff, and he went out of his way to help us anyway he could.

I remember Dr. Victor Crawford encouraging me to continuing my education, he said I was too smart to just be a dental assistant working for him; and that I should go back to school and earn my degree. I took his advice and started taking college courses again in hopes of completing my degree in dental hygiene.

I was working six days a week, going to school part time and taking care of my son. I was trying to do it all, I had no reason to think that my schedule was too much to take on. I was working about 52 hours a week or so, at this time the dental office was open from 8 am until 6 pm during the week and from 8 am till noon on Saturdays. I was also hanging out after work going to the club and probably getting maybe 4 hours of sleep at least 3 times weekly.

I didn't notice that my schedule was over the top, nor could I see that I started to become restless and unable to sleep at night. My brain was working in tenth gear, and I wasn't aware of it. I never called off from work, I was always on time. I hadn't even taken any days off for any personal reason; my son was being cared for by my oldest sister while I was at work, so I didn't think about doing anything but working. I never really seen people that were working class examples in my upbringing on a regular basis. Don't get me wrong some people around me worked in the military, however in my house growing up; not so much. I never witnessed what holding a job and taking care of your family looked like every day; year after year. I had no point of reference of taking vacations, so you don't get burned out, nor did I understand slowing down and pacing myself. I didn't know that I couldn't keep up, until I couldn't keep up!

I found myself not sleeping, becoming confused, hearing voices and seeing things that weren't there. I didn't know this was happening to me again, and I had no ability to catch what happened next.

I lived in La Mesa, and my older middle sister lived with me with two of her three children. I had a boyfriend that lived with me also, he was out to sea due to being in the military. My family noticed that my behavior was unlike me. I was walking around the apartment singing gospel songs, not that, that was out of sorts; but at the time I wasn't actively living my life for God nor was I attending church regularly. My family tried to help me by coming over and trying to convince me to go to the hospital, they sensed that I was on the road to having another mental break and they didn't want me to harm myself nor anyone else. I wouldn't go with them to the hospital, so they called the police in an attempt of getting me help. When the authorities arrived, I went into legal beagle mode and was very calm, professional, and extremely articulate and told the police that there was nothing wrong with me, and I didn't invite my family over my house, and I wasn't in need of medical attention. The police explained to my loved ones that they didn't see anything wrong with me, and I wasn't being harmful to myself nor anyone else; they also made it clear that they didn't see any behavior that suggested that I needed to be hospitalized...therefore they left.

Later that night leading into the morning my thoughts were all over the place and I wasn't sleeping. My son was five years old, and he was sleeping in my room with me because my sister and her children were in his room. I remember having thoughts of someone chasing me and me becoming overly protective of my son; my son woke up and he was on his way to use the bathroom and I remember embracing him and holding him tight to me, and I wouldn't let him go. He kept saying mom I need to use the bathroom, and I was out of my normal senses, and I was overtaken with panic and fear, so I tried to convince him to go ahead and use the bathroom while I was holding him tight in my arms. Thankfully my sister woke up and overheard my son pleading with me to let him go so he could go to the bathroom, she came into the room and freed him from the delusional state that I had slipped into. I don't remember what she said to get him from my embrace, however she was able to take him from me. At the time we did not have a landline phone service in my apartment, and cell phones were non-existent, there were car phones, but only for the rich and famous. My sister gathered her two children and my son and took one of my two cars and headed to the pay-phone on the corner at the 7-eleven to call my mom for help.

During the time that my sister went for help, I started to have this over whelming feeling that God was sending me a message to go to my church and confront the people there for their wrong-doing. My church was off of 43rd Street. My sister took my keys to my other car that was parked in my driveway. I proceeded to walk from Schoolridge Lane in La Mesa, up the hill and entered the 94 going west freeway ramp to get to my church in rush hour morning traffic. I had no control over what I was thinking or doing, I remember most of the details, however I had no ability to recognize that my thoughts and actions didn't make sense, let alone the where with all to stop what I was doing and ask for help. I was having another episode and the sad part was I didn't even know it. My thoughts were in and out, once again. My brain had turned on me and I couldn't help myself, nor was anyone able to pull me out of this downward pit that I found myself to be headed for.

As I walked on the 94 freeway, cars were buzzing passed me, before I left the house; I gathered documents and pictures of my family and shoved them into my white and tan back-pack purse, and I remember wearing this mustard color sweater dress with sandals. I'm recalling these details one, because my feet now bear the corns from walking miles out of my mind on the freeway, and two there was this force driving me to danger that I didn't even know was there.

People were pulling over to where I was on the freeway and trying to convince me to get into the car with them, I didn't realize that they were concerned for my safety, in my mind these people were strangers and I wasn't getting in the car with strangers; so, I kept walking. I walked and walked until I got onto the 805 going south almost to the exit of 43rd, when a police car pulled over to where I was and the officer was able to convince me to get into the car with him. During this time 1993, a law enforcement officer in his car, meant a sign of safety to me. God allowed whatever that officer said, to reach

Tichamingo and I got in the car and off of the freeway, out of rush hour traffic.

While I was on this trip on the freeway, my family went looking for me. My sister made it back from the phone booth, only to find me not in the apartment where she left me. My sister knocked on our neighbor's door to see if they knew where I was, only to be told that they thought they seen me walking down the street. My mom and sisters called my job to see if I had made it to work, and Dr. Crawford told them no, which was alarming to everyone due to my strong work ethics and professionalism. I believe it was Dr. Crawford or my friend from work that told my family that they thought they seen me walking on the freeway, because someone was causing traffic to be backed up. It was then that my family alerted the police to look for me.

The officer drove me to CMH (County Mental Health) off of Rosecrans Street, only to find out that they had no room for me so he had to drive me to Grossmont Hospital. There I was once again going through the process of being placed on a 72 hour hold due to me needing immediate psychiatric intervention.

What is going on? Why is this reoccurring? I thought this would never happen again. As the days went by and I found myself greeted by the staff at the behavior health ward of the hospital, I'm sure these were the questions my family had for the medical providers. The scene played out like before, my family and friends rushed to the hospital to be at my bedside, trying to understand what no one could believe nor image me going through again. So, the first time yes, I played with something I should not have; with the whole being hypnotized thing; but this time, not so...so why did it happen again?

This hospitalization totally caught me completely off guard, I didn't know that I would need to ever be seen again in the behavior health unity of anybody's hospital. Remember the doctor said I didn't need to be under his care, and he took me off of all of the medication they gave me the first time this happen to me. I trusted what they said, my family trusted what they told us as well. Someone didn't give us all the facts, or either they did, and something went terribly wrong. Who or what is behind this cruel sentence that has been placed into my life, and why would someone allow this to repeat itself? I never had the nerve to question God about why this mental health tragedy was playing out in my life, I don't know if it was solely due to my Christian belief system, or due to me being so out of it and then returning to my sanity that I was just happy to know who I was again? Could that be why I didn't ponder, why me? I don't know, now that I'm retelling my experience, I can honestly say that I'm okay with asking God, why did this happen to me? Even as I pose this question, to me the most important question isn't why this happened to me, but who can I help with my story? I desire to answer questions indirectly for someone trying to process understanding mental health and the long- term extensions that steam from the depth of the tentacles of its reach. The arm of which grab you and pull you into a godforsaken place that only

God can touch. The human touch can never reach anyone that has slide into this bleak winding narrow, unknown place of obscurity. This place is or may be indescribable with human language, however I believe that there are many people that have visited this place at least once in their lifetime, or if they keep on living, they may brush shoulders with a certain level of its components. No one willing will enter, especially if you felt the true pain and darkness of it; however, slips into it, or a shove from your circumstances may cause one to see the effects of its hold. However, you come into contact with this place, once you realize where you are, and you are able to sense it; most will try to undo whatever it was that landed you there. Some don't regain their right mind; some enter in and never find the light that leads out. That is because the light has to find you and remove you from that place.

When I went to the hospital this time, I was armed with a point of reference, because I had been here before. The aching muscles from the extreme fatigue, the never-ending shadow of the pale grey, and the fact of losing a part of me was back; this time I knew that once I realized what occurred to me, I had to find some relief that actually worked. While in the locked unit, I went to the group sessions that meant that I was getting better. My family came to the hospital again, and yet again I pleaded with them to take me home each time they came to see me. I used my son as a source of strength to get out of there, so I could see him grow into manhood. I had to get home, to me.

I was in the hospital about two weeks, then I was released. I went to a follow-up appointment with a new doctor, and he prescribed me the same medications that the first doctor had taken me off of. I remember coming home and I had to stay with my mom for a little while so she could look after me and my son. I wasn't strong enough to handle the day-to-day events of everyday life, once again my support system of my mom, and my two sisters kicked in. By this time my mom was married to her third husband, and he allowed my mom to help me during my time of need; and I am most grateful for all of my families loving care.

I stayed with my mom for maybe two weeks, and I was getting better, so I returned to my apartment, and I went back to work; but I had to have my mom keep my son with her for a little longer. My son started attending kindergarten in El Cajon where my mom lived, and I had him on the weekends. This set-up didn't last for long due to me having a hard time working. I ended up getting my son back with me probably after a month or so of him staying with my mom. I was struggling at work, I started noticing that the stress of performance of work responsibilities and duties were difficult. I didn't know that's what it was at the time, now I do. Someone suggested to my mom that I should consider applying for disability from the social security office. My mom went through the paperwork process on my behalf, only for me to be denied. I tried to work, and I couldn't. I continued to try and work as best as I could.

I'm uncertain if the trauma of what I went through the first and now the second time had rendered me in a place of needing either more time working through everything, or what; I wasn't able to tell the difference at that time. I distinctively remember there being physical and mental challenges that were not present prior to 1990.

I was faced with this, oh no, not you again situation in my life; of which there was always this feeling of wondering if I was going to get sick again. The most debilitating part of it all, was I never knew when it was going to happen before it occurred.

The Other Side of Healing

CHAPTER 8

THE MISSING LINK

T ime is going on and I find myself entering into a new relationship with someone that made a large impact in my life. It is 1995 and I kept trying to work despite my concentration being off, and my stress levels becoming harder to manage daily. One day at work, the pressure was intensifying so thankfully I was able to talk to my employer Dr. Crawford, and he signed the paperwork for me to receive short term disability through my job. I remember the benefits from my job ending after a few months and I had to go on public assistance to take care of myself and my son. I didn't want to be on public assistance, I wanted to work. I wanted to be back at work so bad that one day I put on my scrubs and walked around that whole day desiring to be back at work.

The thought of me not being able to hold down a job made me feel like I wasn't contributing to society and there were times I felt down. I was never the type of person that tried to keep up with what others were doing, I just wanted something more meaningful to do with my time that also allowed me to earn an income. I hated being on public assistance with a profound hatred, however that was the only resource available to 24-year-old women with a 7-year-old son. I wasn't receiving any financial support from my son's father that now lived 3000 miles away, and we needed to eat and have a place to stay.

Welfare wasn't much, however it provided what we needed and for that I had to be thankful. I came to terms with the fact that I needed help, so my pride was faced with humility, so I had to bow down and accept the help. No one would have ever known that I was on public assistance, and it wasn't their business to know either; I always had a car, and I paid my bills on time. On top of budgeting my money right, I had a boyfriend that looked after my son and myself as well.

Many people don't understand that there are so many changes you go through while dealing with mental health problems; socially, emotionally, physically, and mentally. One thing is connected to the next, and if or when any of these elements are altered in anyway...the rest falls down like the domino effect. When a crisis occurs, it's just that a full-fledged crisis that no one can foresee, nor make better. It can take years to recover from such a situation, let alone if you keep having disruptions happening in your life.

When I entered this new relationship, the day I met him, just happened to be the same day that I ended my employment. He was in the military, and I met him over my oldest middle sister's place. I had to move in with my mom and her husband, and they lived in the same apartment complex that my sister lived in.

It was a Friday, and I was feeling a little sad about having to come off the job, however I didn't say anything to anybody; I just internalized my feelings trying to cope the best I could. I walked across the parking lot to my sister's place, and she had company. It was never a big deal for a house full of people to be hanging out, my family enjoyed having large crowds of people around us. My son was playing with his cousins riding his bike and he ran over the poor man's foot as I was entering my sister's apartment. I remember saying hello to everyone as I took a seat on the couch, and immediately my eyes locked on this handsome gentleman, and he had the nicest teeth and a cool personality to match. We began conversating with one another and ending up talking all night long. At some point during our delightful exchange, we exchanged phone numbers; my son was walking by on his way back in the room with the rest of the children and seen what was going down and he said, "my momma already got a man!" I looked over at my son, and me and this new beau just laughed.

I started hanging out with this man and we were always together, we eventually moved in a place of our own and worked really good with one another. My family absolutely loved him; he was just that type of person. He was easy to live with and he provided me with anything I could possibly need in a mate. He was born in Brooklyn, NYC and grew up in Atlanta, GA; he is Jamaican with a lovely family that I bounded with well.

I shared my experience with him and tried to explain what I been through as best as I could, that wasn't something I left out when I met people; honesty is what I have always been about. When you talk things out, it allows no room for deception. If someone has the option of being able to decide if they want to continue dating after I have told them about my health history, it makes it easier down the road of the relationship. He didn't express any concerns about my health, so we went on with life.

Shortly after we started seeing one another he had to leave for six months because of his duty with the Navy, this was early into our relationship, and I wasn't looking forward to us being apart. We made the best of his absence and longed to be together, so we wrote to each other regularly. We were only able to talk on the phone a few times during the six months, somehow, we had what it took to maintain our connection.

Before I knew it, he was planning to come back home, and I looked forward to being in his space again. He came home and we continued to strengthen our connection, he spent time with my son making a solid relationship with him at a very vital time in my son's life. Up to this point my son had no real positive male influence in his life, I wasn't aware of this fact at the time, looking back I see it. My son bounded with him to the extent of no one being able to meet the standards that this man provided thereafter.

I remember when my guy took me on a trip to ATL to meet his family for the first time, it was for his niece's high school graduation. I had a great time getting to know his family. Everyone embraced me with such warmth that I have never seen before. I believe this really sealed the deal for me, feeling at home with his people; it truly was the best time of my life.

The first year of our relationship went well, we entered into year two and three with being engaged and preparing to relocate with him to ATL. He decided that he would end his military career and move back to where his family was. I had no thoughts about the decision, I believe you can go anywhere in the world with the right person. I wasn't working during this whole time of our relationship; however, I was able to pay half of all the bills with the public assistance I had coming in.

I was seeing a doctor on a regular basis for my medication management for the mental health condition and I tried to exercise, eat properly and get enough rest to help myself as well. We are in 1997 and I still had difficulty with handling stress. At this point in my life, I was in a healthy relationship and things were going well. I wasn't able to secure employment, so my sons grandma encouraged me to reapply for social security. I wasn't confident in that whole process considering I had been denied twice up to this point. I really didn't understand how they denied me in the first place, I was in need of my disability benefits for various reasons. For one, the public assistance wasn't much to live on and two I started receiving notifications that I had to find a job. There was always this terror of not being able to provide for my son's basic needs; housing, food, and clothing. If it wasn't for the fact that I had a good man in my life that contributed to those needs, I don't know how we would have survived that time of my life.

I decided to follow my son's grandma's advice and I reapplied for my social security benefits again with the help of my doctor. When I went to my appointments, my doctor expressed concern of my inability to gainful be employed; and he also suggested that I apply for social security. He told me that his office would take care of the paperwork that the social security office requested and for me not to worry. With blind trust in a system that had denied me twice was very hard, however I proceeded forward.

To my surprise I was awarded my social security and to top it off they had to back pay me from when my mom had first applied for me! You talking about new found hope in a system that obviously needed reform, that is what this news did for me; it gave me new hope.

I remember receiving my first lump sum check from the social security department, I was shocked to see that they mailed the check in regular mail; thankfully it reached me with no problems.

I was long over- due for having extra of anything, my boyfriend and I use the money to do whatever we wanted. I put some of the money away in the bank only to be told by the social security office that I had to spend the money and I couldn't keep any in the bank or they would cut my monthly stipend. I couldn't believe it, here I was finally trying to regain my financial footing, only to be instructed that

I would be penalized for saving money. I didn't know to buy any property at this time, so I found myself spending all the money.

We had the military pack up our condo and we relocated to ATL. Once we arrived in our new location, I enrolled my son in school and I was able to obtain medical coverage for him through the public assistance program for children, however the state of GA didn't recognize my Medicare red, white, and blue card from the social security administration for medical coverage for myself and they informed me that I would have to pay out of pocket for my medications and care. I never discussed this with my fiancé, I just went on with the information and really didn't think much about not having the resources to pay for my meds and care. I was in love with a great man, and we were headed toward marriage; without a care in the world. I wasn't the effective communicator I am today at that time, and truly wasn't well versed in properly navigating through conflict resolution either; next thing I know we hit a tough part of our relationship.

This was my first time being away from my family for longer than two weeks, and I became home sick for my support system that I left in California. I found myself feeling God tugging on the strings of my heart, and I could not continue to dismiss the dreams and continuous visions that woke me up most nights. I grew up going to church, so I could tell that the Lord was trying to get me back on a path that included Him being in the center of my life.

My guy left the military with a lump sum of money of which we went through along with my lump sum; and he didn't gain employment right away when we relocated and had to ultimately take a job that paid poorly.

I was still able to pay half of all of our household expenses with my social security monthly benefits, however my guy had more going out than coming in. One day while we were talking, my guy told me, "I couldn't live out my life on no government fantasy, and I needed to find a job." I was in disbelief, my feelings were hurt; how could he say such harmful words considering that he had no issues helping me spend all of my "government fantasy," money up! I was insulted, but I didn't say anything when he said that I shut down; a week or so later I decided to ship my car back to California and get two one- way tickets back to San Diego for myself and my son. I felt that since my love wasn't enough to bring to the table along with paying half of the household expenses, I would go back home.

I lived in Atlanta for 9 months without any psyche medication and care from a doctor. My connection with my guy was so tight, that he expressed out of his own mouth and heart that all I needed was him; without any real understanding of my mental health condition and my need for continual medication and care. I didn't know that I couldn't or shouldn't go without my medications and care, so I never realized what was happening to my mind and body on a chemical level when I didn't have it in my system. I was completely under educated on my newfound health situation, even though it was 7 years after my first mental break crisis. I tucked my emotional baggage inside of me and headed back to Callie. Whenever I felt uneasy in a relationship, I would get as far away from the situation as I could; rather it was by putting some distance between myself and the person or cutting communication off completely...I would go on about my business without explanation. I believe this was the way I kept from falling apart; I felt the effects of this failed relationship despite the fact of not being able to talk through how I felt with my guy. Even though we didn't break up when I left, it was over, and I knew it.

CHAPTER 9

HEED TO THE CALL

When I made it back home to San Diego it was September 1998, I moved in with my mom, her husband, and my little brother. The cost of housing was on the rise, and I couldn't afford to live on my own with the social security money I had coming in. My mom's husband had bought a modest size two-bedroom house in east Daygo on 36th street, I was thankful he opened their doors and allowed my son and myself to share my little brothers room. We made the best out of the situation, as I tried to secure my own housing.

During this time, I was a little withdrawn on the inside, I was tired of hanging out and being in dead in relationships, I felt like there had to be more to life. I was uncertain of what I needed in my life, I just wanted to experience a fresh breath of air. I hadn't been attending church on a consistent basis since I was in high school, however I felt a strong pull in that direction.

One day I was hanging out with some friends, and one of my friends noticed by my conversation that God was dealing with me; this friend was wise enough to encourage me to give my life to the Lord. It was at that point that I realized that I needed a change in my life that would result in me having internal peace.

This may sound as if there was no struggle going from what I was doing in life, into a lifestyle that required me to unlearn years of misguided thinking; on the contrary, I had to embrace more than just going to church. I wasn't concerned about the ins and outs of moving closer to God, there was this feeling of safety that kept me calm. One thing I knew for sure was everyone around me that lived their life for God, always showed me that they had no regrets. The excitement that believers of God expressed, made me desire to have that and more.

One of the best things about moving in with my mom and her family, was the fact of them attending one of the first Apostolic churches in San Diego on 28th and L street; Greater Apostolic Faith Temple Church. Bishop Charles Taylor was the pastor at that time. One night I was hanging with my mom and one of her friends from the church, and I decided to go with them to church that night. I was driving and they were talking about the goodness of the Lord, and I was so overtaken by the spirit of God that I began to worship him and before I knew it, I was speaking in a heavenly language and tears were flowing down my face. My mom's friend had to grab the steering wheel, thankfully we were pulling up to the church by then and we managed to park safely. We went inside for service, and I rededicated my life to the Lord.

I had to make doctor's appointments and reestablish my care when I got back in town. It was about three weeks into me being back home before I actually seen my care providers and got a new prescription for my psyche meds. I began overly associating myself with the bible, and I was having a difficult time sleeping. I was dealing with the change of being in close quarters with my mom and her family, the end of a good relationship, and building my personal relationship with God. You take all of that and add it to the fact of being without medication for 9 months and you have a downward spiral on your hands, all of which I was not aware of. One thing I noticed with being on the verge of a mental breakdown was, my episodes caused me to be deep in thought or sensitive to things related to what I call the supernatural. I notice that now, however I could never tell when I was getting sick. I'm sure people around me could tell, my behavior would change. I would do things that were out of character, or irrational. I had no mechanism inside of me that warned me about what I was doing nor thinking, that is scary. Over the years of me dealing with my experience, I have come across other people that have had mental break downs; it's amazing how people that have never experienced this on a personal level think that people are faking it. Who would fake walking around seeing things that aren't there? You have to be a real diabolic person to intentionally pretend to have something wrong with you, when there is nothing wrong with you; that usually means that you do have deep seated issues. What I'm saying is this, I am not the person that would even want to pretend something is wrong with me, I'm not interested in being the center of attention. When I have slipped out of reality, I couldn't brace myself for everything that followed. How do you prepare for the unwanted, is there such a thing?

I had applied for a job at the post office during this time, it just so happens that there were multiple openings that needed to be filled; so, they had a massive hiring event. My middle oldest sister and I both got offered a job and we were scheduled to go to our orientation the same day and time. We had to travel 30 minutes north of San Diego for our training, and I was the one driving us to our appointment. As we were driving on 805 north, I became disoriented and confused; a drive that should have been no longer than 30 minutes turned into 1 hour and 45 minutes. My sister kept trying to get me to pull over and let her drive, to no avail. I didn't realize that I was in danger of losing my mind, I was driving around in circles. Needless to say, we were extremely late for our appointment, and missed an employment opportunity. Somehow, we made it back to San Diego without any harm to us, I'm sure my sister told my mom that I was getting sick again.

On the day I had my appointment to go see my doctor, my mom and her friend from church took me. My son was 10 years old, and he went with me to my appointment. The night before, I was up all night, hearing voices, and seeing things that weren't there. The voices sounded like an old radio station that wasn't coming in clear, the frequency was distorted with an overlapping of multiple people talking all at the same time. My son tried to comfort me and get me to go to sleep, can you imagine a child watching his mom experience something that he has seen before, and had no way of helping; He did what he thought would help, which was to stick close by me during those night terrors. When we arrived at the Euclid medical center, we went inside the building and took the elevator to the third floor to the doctor's office. During the appointment, I don't recall much; this appointment was designed to play what I call the medication game; which consisted of me going to get a prescription for my psyche meds. The game goes like this, you come to your appointments, and you get your needed medication, you miss your appointments, you don't get what you need. I know the appointments are designed for the providers to monitor their patients and ensure that the medications are being taken properly, and to see how the patient is doing while taken them. I am thankful for health care providers, at this point of my journey; my health literacy wasn't what it is today. I read and understood fine, my problem was that It never dawned on me that I had a condition that wouldn't just end once I was out of the hospital. I never seen myself as a person that needed continuous care. This perspective I had was probably fostered from being young and not understanding that mental health was as normal as my physical or spiritual health.

I told the doctor that I had moved out of the state and was without medication for 9 months, the appointment ended with the doctor giving me a prescription that I needed to have filled immediately. My family was hoping that by me getting my medication, everything would be fine. I'm sure they didn't want to see me go through what I did with my first nor second psychotic break. No one realized how bad off I was, but we were getting ready to find out.

After my son and I left out of the appointment, we were supposed to get on the elevator and go to the basement level of the building to where the pharmacy was located, I became confused and turned around. I was walking without knowing where I was and I didn't even know where I was supposed to be, just wondering in bewilderment. My son took my hand and he tried to guide me to where he thought we needed to go, thankfully my mom and her friend entered the building and seen how confused I was; they took me to get my medication, then we went back to my mom's house.

When we got back to my mom's house, I remember sitting on the porch with my little brother; then I turned on the water hose and proceeded to drench myself while I was fully clothed. My mom came outside and told me to get out of the water and go take off my wet clothes. I was helpless, and in need of desperate psychiatric attention. My mom's friend was trying to help my mom with me, and I'm sure they were hoping that my medication would kick in and save me from slipping into another dark mental pit. I had a conversation with my mom's friend about the Yin and Yang; of which I had never even heard of at the time, nor had I done any research on the subject matter. Where the knowledge of what we were discussing came from, I don't know, all I know is in 1998 I was telling her about the world going to a cashless society that used a different form of currency, and everyone would use the one world system.   Recently when the global pandemic of the Corona Virus hit the world in 2019, I had a conversation with my mom's friend, and she reminded me of some of what we talked about in 1998. Most of what we discussed then has been forever lost with time, however we both remember certain aspects of what I told her, and we both have lived to see the system in place that uses different currency methods that are vastly approaching a cashless society.

As the evening went into bedtime, my disposition grew worse and my mom had to call the emergency squad to come transport me to the behavior health side of Grossmont hospital for the third time in my life. This hospitalization was bad, all bad. My thoughts were scrambled, and I couldn't maintain anything that resembled reality.

My first and second breakdown caused me to be in the hospital for about two weeks or so, this time it was more like a month or more. It was as if I were living out a bad scene in a movie that kept rewinding to the same place. Each time I visited Grossmont behavior health, I experienced being stripped down to nothingness. My mind was out in a place of its own, that didn't have a guarantee of a return to my norm. These hospitalizations were happening back-to-back, 1990, 1993, and now 1998; and it was taking a toll on everything about me. The 90's were tough for me, and everyone connected to me. I should have been enjoying college, and everything that goes along with the coming-of-age story line, instead I was fighting an unknown battle to stay sane. Imagine fighting a fight when you are not armed with the right tools to win, I had to learn how to be able to help myself to have a chance of not being knocked down over and over again.

Once again, my family and friends came to see about me while in the hospital. I started off in the unlocked unit, and once again that ended with me in need of being in the locked unit. One of my friends that I was hanging with real tough at the time, I use to affectionately call her Tac-head; because she was drop dead fine and she and I would roam around town in boxer shorts and sports bra's, her hair was so beautiful, but often she would just pull it into a bun...so I gave her that nick-name. When my friend made it to the hospital, my mom told her to pull herself together before she came to see me, because she was emotionally distraught to see me in such a bizarre state of mind. All she did was cry her eyes out. When she came to visit me, the staff was in the process of cleaning me up, so they told my friend and peer she could give me a shower and dress me. There I was 27 years old, and I couldn't even bathe and dress myself. Who has their close friend give them a shower and put their clothes on them like a little baby? Any form of embarrassment goes out the door when you are out of your natural mind! I didn't even know to be embarrassed. I half-way don't even remember all of the things that my family and friends had to help me with when I became sick.

Another one of my close sister-friends (we have been friends since 3^(rd) grade), came up to the hospital to see me, this time I was using the bathroom doing the number two; and she had to help me wipe my butt! Yucky, nobody wants to wipe no poop off no grown person, but the love of my support system really caused her to step in and help her friend without pause. I often tell this friend that I will always keep her close, because she has too much incriminating info on me!

One day while in the hospital this trip, I had to go to another side of Grossmont for a brain scan; the technician took me over in a wheelchair. Once the tech wheeled me into the room for the test, he left me in the room by myself and I left the room. I was wondering around the hospital campus confused and paranoid. I had thoughts of someone chasing me, so I was trying to escape and leave. I made it to a different area of the hospital and managed to make two phone calls. The first call was to my homeboys from East St. Louis they were dudes that didn't play around with the street life, when X picked up the phone; I told him that someone was after me and I needed them to come get me. X called the rest of the crew and told them that they were going on a "Who" ride to go handle these people that were chasing after me. One of the homies, had enough sense to say, "let me call Tichamingo's mom, because I think she is in the hospital." Sure, enough he verified with my mom that I was in the hospital, and my mom told them to call off the posse.

The other call I made was to my mom to tell her that I was running away from the hospital, and I needed her to come get me. My mom kept me on the phone trying to figure out where I was. While my mom was on the phone with me another call beeped in (call waiting on a landline), it was the hospital informing my mom that they didn't know my whereabouts. My mom told them that I was on the other end of the phone, and that I was still at the hospital somewhere, but she didn't know where; and I was so confused that I couldn't tell my mom exactly where I was. The nurse on the phone put out an alert on the overhead speaker in the hospital, and shortly after that the staff members found me on the other side of the hospital, far away from where I was supposed to be.

When I realized where I was, I had to focus on getting better so I could get out of the hospital and go home to my loved ones; and once again I thought about my son, and I used my love for him to get me back in a healthier place.

This time, I couldn't ignore this reoccurring event of my life. I had to learn all I could, considering that I found myself here once more. It was time for me to look into this condition a little closer. My doctor suggested that I try being around others that were going through a similar experience.

When I got out of the hospital, I signed myself up for outpatient group therapy and I went three days a week. The sessions were facilitated by the behavior health staff members of Grossmont hospital. This was a very interesting way to find out about how to help myself, at least in theory. I remember my first group session, and I gotta say; I left there feeling worse.

While I was in the group session listening to other people talk about their problems, it was depressing. Many of the participants had backgrounds that would bring anyone with a heart to tears. I arranged to use the transportation system they offered while attending the group sessions, in an effort to save money from not using my own vehicle. They provided us with a meal voucher to cover for our lunch and honestly that was the highlight of my day; eating a good lunch. For the most part that was all I learned from those sessions, I suppose if I looked deeper; I could say that I learned that many people had mental health conditions related to events that occurred in their lives. Most people had drug problems that caused the mental conditions, that I'm sure were connected to traumatic events; Some people experienced mental disturbances from day one of their lives; then you had a few people that fell into a category of having come in contact with a mind -altering experience that resulted in a mental health problem. Whatever landed a person in search for coping skills to help them, it didn't matter; we all wanted to be better.

I didn't go far with my group therapy sessions, like I said it was depressing; I couldn't stand to be in that environment. It wasn't healthy for me; it could have been due to how vulnerable I was; or perhaps it just wasn't what I needed. If I have learned anything on my path into the management of my mental health; you must do what works best for you; and often you have to try different methods of help before finding the right fit. The process of discovering what works best is at times, trial and error. If you come across the wrong method, at the wrong time; it could result in going backwards with your care. It's hard sticking to things that take a while of you trying it out, before you realize that it's not working.

I have heard many people talk about why they stop taken their medications, mostly because it makes you feel sleepy, or unlike you with no drive or desire to do anything. In my case, the main reason I would come off my medications, is because I didn't think I needed them. I thought that if I took care of myself by staying happy, then I wouldn't need to use any medications. It doesn't matter how hard you try to, "will" something to go away with using mind over matter; that is a bunch on nonsense. What I'm about to say doesn't apply for everyone; it applies to me; I needed the help of being on medications on a daily basis. I had to heed to the call of becoming someone who learned about mental health and how I wanted my life to be; and I had to take responsibility for my own care. If I didn't start somewhere with dealing with my condition, I would have continued revisiting that dreadful behavior hospital. Dreadful, from the point of view of not wanting to be sick, not from the perspective of not receiving the care I needed.

Although I wasn't in ATL any longer, when my guy found out I had a break down, he was hurt because he wasn't there for me to help me through the situation. He and I tried to do the long- distance relationship thing, it didn't work. We officially broke it off in 2000. The relationship I had with him was the longest and best relationship I have had on record, to this day we still keep in contact and have a mutual respect for one another that no one can take from us. His mom and I also are very supportive of one another, and we have kept in touch over the years, we make sure we talk regularly as well.

In 1999, I was having a difficult time managing my stress levels, my thoughts began to race, and I became fearful of having a breakdown; so, I went to Grossmont hospital and checked myself into the hospital to get some help. I had a lot going on: church, family life, and trying to manage my care. After I started attending church on a regular basis, I became very depressed, this depression ended up lasting the whole year. I never experienced depression for that long before, and I haven't since then either. This was the first time I went to the hospital for my mental health, and I didn't have a full-blown break-down. I stayed in the hospital for only 1 week, and once I was released, I continued going to the doctor on a regular basis and taking my medications like I was supposed to. I stop going to the physical building for church, however I would spend countless hours praying, studying and reading my bible. I had a Gideon bible that I got from one of my hospital visits, and a pocket dictionary from the 99-cent store;

and the Lord revealed Himself to me. One of my friends from church would call me every time she was at church and didn't see me. She would call and say, "are you coming to church today?" my reply was, no not today. She continued checking on me and encouraging me to come to church throughout the remainder of the year.

I had enough strength to make sure my son got up for school and ate. He was in middle school, and after 1 year of living with my mom and her family I was able to get an apartment in El Cajon that was based on my income. My son, I'm sure noticed how withdrawn I was, even though we never talked about my mental health situation; he probably was left to deal with life the best way he could. I was able to maintain our monthly household expenses and keep food and shelter in place. I hit a new place with my mental health, I thought I was doing better with my care and I was; there was still so many different levels of what I endured, that I may never be able to express how deep my condition negatively changed my existence.

CHAPTER 10

70 x 7

A fter I spent one year in a depressed state, I started attending church again. Every time the doors of the church were open, I made it my business to be there. I needed something that gave me hope, up to this point in my life, I felt as though this was the best decision for me. I would go up to the church for prayer, choir rehearsal, bible study, Sunday school, morning worship, and any other services that kept me focused on God and not much of anything else.

The first Sunday of me going back to church I met a brother that was from Arizona. We started dating and ended up getting married. I began to learn what I thought was the right and wrong way to have a successful relationship, it seemed to me that when I came closer to God, I gave certain personality types more of a chance than what they deserved. This brother from the start was damaged goods, he had me in the pastor's office almost every day of us being together. He had unresolved issues from his past, that didn't work for me, and it wasn't the right combination nor connection. I could give you details about what occurred while I was in this relationship, however I will stick to explaining the importance and power of forgiveness.

Forgiveness is so simplistic that it is often missed used or not used at all. I had to learn first- hand that when you take steps to forgive someone, it is always for the person that has been done wrong. True forgiveness will challenge your thinking and place you in a situation where you have to deal with everything surrounding releasing the person; in order for you to be at peace. It wasn't until I started reading the Bible that I truly understood why you must forgive. The bottom-line to forgiveness is, the fact of needing to be forgiven daily for things that we do. This was a concept that people around me used, however it wasn't until I spent years studying the subject matter; that I personally recognized how to tap into its power for myself. There are many layers to how deep you go into exercising forgiveness; the depth is contingent upon how bad the situation is. For example; if someone has betrayed your trust; you may need more time working through how to forgive them; it will depend on if you have experienced broken trust issues before. You will also have to take a look at how you process what has occurred to you. Life has a way of making you deal with things sooner instead of allowing time to go by without dealing with how you feel. I had to learn how to allow myself to address emotions behind what I felt, this wasn't easy. Usually, I would get as far away from whatever the issue was and never directly unpack what happened. This method worked, however; I had to look back years later and institute healthier communication if I ever wanted to be in the position where I resolved conflict immediately.

I have always known that I couldn't allow anything to interfere with the peace I have in my heart, that is one reason I chose to forgive.

When I began to explore what true forgiveness looked like, I found out that you don't have to allow yourself to be anybody's door mat. Meaning, when you forgive, you don't have to continue to be around the person; often you have to distance yourself from the individual. When you become stronger, if you have to be around the person; for example; if it's a family member; you can. Time is the best method to use with forgiveness; it's case by case, and no one can dictate the duration but you. If you find yourself feeling uneasy, or angry when you are around the person you have forgiven; you probably need more time working on forgiveness. For me, when you can be in the same space with someone you have forgiven, and you don't even blink at them funny; then you probably have truly let them go and you are no longer holding any ill towards them.

The most beneficial part of forgiveness is honesty. Stay in tune with how you feel and be honest with your feelings. Never try to put on a fake facade in front of others; if you not feeling the individual, then take the time you need. Never rush the process, it will not get you closer to forgiving the person. When you come in contact with people that have no clue of how to deal with their issues, it will cause a breakdown in the communication process. If we are honest, we all have things that we can improve upon in our connections with others, some people don't have the skill set to address their problems in a healthy manner. I believe that you can become a better person if you seek out help. Often people don't want others to know what they feel, and how they behave behind closed doors. Some people try to use the word of God as a control device, to lord over others. The Bible is supposed to be used as your individual guide to help you become a better person; work on yourself and stop trying to tell others what they need to change. When you apply principles in the bible properly, the world around you will be different, why; because you view things differently. I'm grateful that God gave me a good sense of my worth, and I was able to cut my loses and leave the situation. No one gets married thinking they will divorce, unfortunately things didn't pan out, and it was best to move on. So, I found myself in yet another failed relationship. I got married trying to do what I thought the bible was teaching me to do, however looking back; I didn't get married for the right reason and I didn't understand what the bible had to say about the subject matter. This relationship ended with me having a need for major change, after being back in San Diego for seven years, I had enough, and I moved to the state where I was born; Ohio. In fact, my mom and her family, my middle sister and her children and eventually my oldest sister and her children relocated to Ohio as well.

There was a storm that blew me into Columbus, Ohio; and I was happy to have the chance to be in a new environment with a clean slate. I was still working on a two-year college degree, and my school was located near where I leaved. I arrived in town January 2005 and started attending the Apostolic church my mom was going to. There was a big difference in the churches in Ohio in comparison to the liberal congregations on the west coast. Church people in Ohio wanted to see what your spiritual pedigree was; as if they could determine that by asking millions of questions that have nothing to do with God's plan of salvation...it is crazy how people act as if they are God and can put others in or out of heaven. If it wasn't for my personal relationship with God, and the fact of me not caring what others think of me; I may have been offended and left God; due to people.

Even though I sensed that Ohio was strangely different, I embraced my new surroundings and I planted myself into a closer bound with God. There was good leadership and teaching at my new church and I really valued that. I learned about diplomacy, and protocol on a level never seen before. There were solid connections made with the people of God and that helped my transition.

Another aspect of living where I was born, was the hope of me finding out about my family on my father's side. I was in contact with my father by letter only, due to him being in prison; and he never gave me any information about other members of his family; with the exception of a sister that I was in contact with that lived in Maryland. More recently I was able to meet my father in person and more of my family on my father's side and establish a relationship with some of them, this included an older brother; I feel thankful for these connections. Shortly after I seen my father as an adult, he passed away; I don't take it for granted that I was able to spend time with my father prior to him passing. There is a smile on my face, that will always be there just because I was able to see my father and get to know him.

I worked so hard with trying to complete my goal of completing my dental hygiene degree. I started this pursuit back in 1990 and it was a very long road. I was on campus one day, and I met this fella. We started hanging out and after a year of us meeting; we got married. He was family oriented, and he was a very intelligent man. Once again, I will not go into the details of our relationship; but I want to explain the misconception that most faith believers have about being "saved," and having a mental health condition.

I'm going to church, loving God and enjoying my 2nd marriage. This was the first time that I was extremely close to God, as an adult and doing all of what I thought it took to maintain my connection to Him. I was praying, reading my bible, paying my tithes; and practicing all the other tenants of my faith; as I had learned to do. I never thought about the emotional connection to others, and I didn't realize when these connections are not aligned properly; that there will be a mental imbalance that follows. My spouse and I did not have a harmonious relationship; matter of fact he turned the light switch off on me right after we were married, and I shut down. I had never experienced rejection before with any other relationship and it was painful to find myself at 33 years of age experiencing this emotion for the first time. I never knew someone could love you while simultaneously treating you mean. One minute he told me how much he cared for me, then in the same breath he would go off on me without cause or reason.

I never was the type to sit back and take no mess from someone that was my mate, or anyone else for that matter. To find myself in a textbook situation with someone harming me verbally; I couldn't wrap my brain around his unstable behavior. Once again looking back, God told me not to marry him, I felt the guilt and shame of sin and married him. More importantly, I needed to look closer to what was inside of myself that caused me to do the opposite of what God instructed me to do. That was probably the biggest lesson learned from both of my failed marriages.

Eight months after my second husband and I were married, the pressure and stress of our relationship had taken its toll on me and I broke down. I started hearing voices and became delusional. I had no control over my actions, and I wasn't able to express my need of help.

On the day that I was hospitalized, my mom I believe picked up on the fact of me getting sick. My husband was at work and my mom stopped by to check on me. When my mom arrived at my house, it took me about ten minutes to open the door for her, I was out of it; zoning in and out once again into the dark place of mental torment and anguish. I snapped out of the disparity of listlessness long enough to realize my mom was at the door, and I opened the door for her. When my mom entered the home, she had two toddlers with her that she was babysitting for; she sat the children down and noticed that I had lost control of my bladder and was soaked with pee; she instructed me to go change. My mom had to come in my room and help me due to me being confused, and I couldn't understand what she had told me to do. I was mumbling words that my mom couldn't make out, and I was pacing back and forth. My mom found me some clothes to put on, and she called my husband at work and told him that I needed to go to the hospital. My husband came straight home. When he made it to our house, he rudely put my mom and the two children out of the house on the front porch and slammed the door in her face and told her that he would take care of his wife.

My husband managed to get me in his car, and he drove me to the nearest hospital. My mom was trying to help my husband get me the care I needed considering that this was his first time going through something like this; he wouldn't hear of it and did what he thought was best. My husband took me to Mt. Carmel East, and when we arrived; they evaluated me and determined that I needed immediate behavior health services.

My family came up to the hospital to see what was going on, and of course by now my mom had told them that my husband put her out the house and wouldn't let her help him. My family didn't know for sure that her took me to Mt. Carmel East, however since that was the closes hospital to where we lived; they showed up there. It was a bad situation; my family was ready to beat down my husband; the only thing that saved him from my family was the fact of him alerting security at the hospital. He had my family removed from the premises.

My Pastor, his son (of whom I am close with), and my assistant Pastor; came up to the hospital in hope of offering prayer and support to my family. My mom was distraught, and she informed them of how my husband was behaving, before they were escorted away from the hospital. My oldest sister was so angry, she cussed my husband out in front of my Pastor; it was a volatile scenario.

Before my family was ordered off of the hospital grounds, my Pastor, assistant Pastor, and my Pastor's son prayed for me; I remember zoning in and out while they were by my bedside. My head was spinning into a place that hurts, and I wasn't able to comprehend what was occurring to me. I'm thankful that my Pastor is known for being a leader that believes in visiting the sick and praying for them.

My husband wasn't cooperating with anyone in my family, not even my son. My son was so hurt behind what was happening to me that he called his father, and his father came to be with him. My son's father doesn't play when it comes to his loved ones, and they wanted to do whatever it took to straighten my husband out; thankfully my oldest sister told them not to harm my husband because he still had the legal say so over me. Everyone in my support system had to pull back and pray to God that everything worked out for me.

After everyone from my support system left the hospital, Mt. Carmel East informed my husband that I needed to be transported to their hospital on the west side of Columbus, because that is where they have behavior health services. My husband allowed them to transport me to the other hospital, which was what needed to be done; however, he didn't tell my family that they moved me.

The next day after I was moved to Mt. Carmel West hospital, my mom called Mt. Carmel East; and they wouldn't give her any information about me; however, they told her that no one by my name was in their hospital. My mom's worst fears were unfolding; she called our Pastor, and our assistant Pastor to inform them; our assistant Pastor reached out to my husband, in hopes that his connection with my husband would prompt him to hear the voice of reason; and let my family know where I was. I thank God for everyone that was praying for me and my family during this whole ordeal, because I know without doubt that this could have been worse.

I'm uncertain of what exactly was said to my husband, when my assistant Pastor talked to him, but my family was informed of my where abouts; and they began to come to Mt. Carmel West to check on me.

My husband was concerned about me, I believe he didn't know what to do; he came to the hospital every day that I was hospitalized. I remember, after I would have my dinner, I would see him walking down the street to come see me. There was this large window in the area of Mt. Carmel West where the patients in the hospital could look outside, and he couldn't see me, but I would see him as he made the attempt to come see about me. If I were to put myself in his shoes, I imagine I would be at a loss of what is the right way to handle such a delicate situation as well.

I wasn't privy to the backdrop of the feuding going on between my family and my husband; and I'm glad they protected me from knowing all of the details, it would have made my recovery even more difficult.

My son had access to my bank account and I remember during this time my husband informed me that all of my money had been withdrawn from my account; it was around the beginning of the month and bills were due; my husband had access to my account as well, and he was attempting to meet our household obligations; only to find out that there was no money for him to take out. Your probably thinking, "why did my son have access to my account?" Let me explain, when my husband and I got married, my husband's credit was bad and he had recently filed for bankruptcy prior to us getting married, and we couldn't add him to my banking institutions account; but he was able to add me to his. I didn't reroute my direct deposits, due to me having money from California coming in. Therefore, I had money taken out of my primary account into the account my husband and I had for our household expenses, (I was still paying half of everything with my social security benefits). My son had one of my debit cards, and my husband had my wallet that had the other debit card in it. When my automatic draft didn't reach the account my husband and I had together, he told me about it while I was in the hospital.

When my son, his father and his brother came to the hospital to see me, I asked my son to put my money back in my account so that my account wouldn't be charged an overdraft fee; my son told me he took the money out because he didn't know what my husband was planning on doing, and he didn't want him to take my money from me. I was appreciative that my son was safeguarding his mom, he put the money back into the account and everything worked out.

I don't recall how long I was in the hospital for this episode, but this was the worst breakdown of them all. It was the worse breakdown because the effects of it impacted my life the longest.

When I was released from the hospital, I was still married; and I had to deal with everything that lead up to me having the breakdown in the first place. I got married to my second husband in September of 2006, I had the breakdown in May of 2007.

Once I came home with my husband, we tried to move forward in our relationship; I never asked God to get me out of the situation, I continued to pour out my heart to God on behave of my husband. I prayed that the Lord would help my husband with whatever it was between us that caused him to chew me up one side, and express and profess his love for me at the same time. I started going to therapy, seeking help to try and understand what I was doing wrong, and how I could change to be whatever was needed in order for me to be the wife my husband needed. This relationship hit me hard, and left me feeling as though something was wrong with me. My self -worth and self- esteem needed healing and repair.

There was this misconception in the black church that, suggested that if you are living your life for the Lord and doing what you are supposed to be doing; that you wouldn't, or shouldn't experience any mental health issues. I have been told by people of faith on more than one occasion that, "people with the Holy Ghost, shouldn't have break downs, and if they do; they must not be trusting God!" I have always known from my personal experience with mental health issues, that it has nothing to do with a person having the Holy Ghost or not! It has more so to do with time and chance happening to us all than anything else.

I think of the story of Job in the bible, he was a man that did everything he was supposed to do and expected to do from God's point of view and yet he experienced devastation after devastation. He lost all of his children in the same day to a tragic natural disaster, as well as being robbed of his oxen and camels, and some of his employees being massacred, and a fire killing his sheep and his other employees; to add further insult, his support system failed him. His friends questioned his faithfulness to God and accused him of not doing what God told him to do; in an attempt of understanding the sudden bad events that were happening to him. This account is one of the best illustrations of the fact that; God allows us to go through things to strengthen our connection to Him; then God will allow us to be used as a witness to others of God's never-ending grace and mercy. We are designed to point people in God's direction, that is one of the main reasons God created us.

One of my favorite examples of how we are to extend forgiveness to each other is in the bible; Jesus was teaching a lesson to the disciples on forgiveness, within this session one of the apostles, Peter, asked Jesus how often he should forgive someone that continues to do him wrong? Peter wanted to put a limit on extending forgiveness, and Jesus corrected his thinking by telling him that we are expected to forgive people seventy times seven; daily. This exaggeration points to the fact, that we should go beyond what we think we can do and enter into a realm of forgiveness that requires God's help to get it done.

CHAPTER 11

SITTING ON THE COUCH OF SELF-HELP

My marriage to my second husband could not withstand the stress of an ectopic pregnancy, a spouse that was narcissistic nor a wife with a schizophrenic diagnosis; it ended with yet another failed divorce.

I separated from my husband February 2008 and cut off all ties by September 2008 when I came to the conclusion that I didn't need any more examples of his bad behavior. I shut down and went into silent broken mode. I lost hope in people. This was the first relationship that I vested everything in me; I learned how to love and accept love; from God, not people. I embraced how God feels about relationships, and I was implementing every principle I could.

Our divorce was finalized in April of 2009, and I had to restructure everything about who I was. I was teaching a small group bible study at my church, we met weekly, and this class saved my life.

I grabbed every book I could get my hands on that dealt with helping yourself heal after a loss. I knew that the pain I felt had to be addressed immediately. I also knew that I was never supposed to allow the hurt to cause me to give up on me.

I dove deeper into studying the bible, and I prepared for my weekly class like my life depended on it! My life needed all the extra help it could get. My support system kicked in with love and concern, like never before, and I was surrounded by my family, friends, and church family in a time that was very critical for me. Most of the people around me, never knew how much I needed them.

My son had his first daughter during this time, and I had to move in with him; this allowed me the opportunity to experience unconditional love on another level. I needed my granddaughter more than she needed me perhaps. While my son worked, I would keep my granddaughter; it was so delightful having a newborn around. She most certainly came in my life at the right time.

There was this movie that told a story of a bird that was displaced from his owner, and he spent his life trying to get back to his owner; In the movie; there was a lullaby that the little girl's mom would sing to her and I fell in love with the lyrics because they reflected what I felt towards me loving my granddaughter the first time, I saw her. I hung onto anything that helped me overcome my heartache.

My process of healing was a long process. When I reflect back, I spent five years of not dating nor entertaining the possibility of being in a relationship; because I needed the time alone with God in order for me to heal properly.

In my opinion, when you encounter a situation that leaves you in a numb and loss mindset; you must try to regain your strength; for me it required me to shut out anything that may harm me further. I was hurt to my core, but I didn't want to be hurt so I cared for myself.

I thank the Lord that I had been in good relationships prior to both of my marriages; so, I knew what a healthy, loving, respectful relationship looked like. I wasn't shy of expressing myself in relationships; what I liked and disliked nor what worked and what didn't. When things didn't work out, I knew how to move on without looking back, and I also wasn't afraid to admit my wrong.

As I was recovering from this failed marriage, I realized It had been 14 years since I was in the workforce; due to my mental health condition. During this time, there were a few times I tried to work, however the stress of working and dealing with life; blocked me from being gainfully employed. I never realized the connections to my inability to work or complete my two-year college degree, with my mental health. While I grieved the loss of my marriage, I applied for a job in the dental field. I needed newfound purpose, and I felt that all I needed was for an employer to give me a chance. I was hired and despite the fact of not working for such a long time, my skill set was still on point; I advanced like I had never left the workforce. It was just what I needed, and I have been moving forward since then. It is amazing how I was going through one of the lowest points of my life, and the doors were open for me to work. I was glad that I had enough money to take care of my expenses, and a couple extra nickels left over as well.

I had been working on a two- year degree since 1990, and it wasn't until 2017 that I understood that my condition had directly held me back from earning my college degree. I spent many years on and off attending college and furthering my education. The years I spent on this relentless pursuit was interwoven with years of trying to come to terms with my mental health.

After my first mental health episode, and the reoccurring breakdowns after that; there were times I would come off of my medication cold turkey, and it never occurred to me that when I did this, the same symptoms the medicine would treat; it caused. What am I saying? When the medicine commercials advise patients to seek their medical doctors advise prior to starting or stopping their medication; believe me when I say, please make sure you listen. I never understood the why, until 2009.

One day I was on the phone with one of my dear friends, and he and I would talk for hours. He was a very smart man of God; and he also had an amazing sense of humor to match. We were in a very intense conversation about this and that; and I was going on and on, jumping from concept to concept; point of view to analysis...when we switched topics and began to touch on the ends and outs of what we were going through. I was explaining to him how I felt about medicine, and being under a doctor's care; I was going on and on; and he shared about his experience with depression, and how he didn't know how to get help...in the middle of our discussion, I was encouraging him to take care of himself; he picked up on an underlining point to what we were taking about and said, "Tichamingo, why don't you just take your medicine?" I was floored with my mouth wide- open, I had never been asked that question! It was of God that he said what he said, but most importantly it took on new meaning for me. Up to this point in my care and navigating through the whole mental health world, I never had the revelation that my balance within my mental state rested on the fact of me taking my medicine regularly.

When I would stop taking my medicine cold turkey, I would start to decline into a delusional, confused state of mind. The medicine caused me to experience hearing voices and seeing things that were not there, why? Because my condition would be that of an altered mental state when I failed to give my brain the extra help it needed to remain in a state of sanity. I will restate what I have tried to convey throughout my account of what happened to me; I respond well to medication treatment for my particular diagnosis, if you find yourself trying to figure out what works best for you; please approach the matter with Godly wisdom and professional care. I will say it again for the hard of understanding people, what works for me, may not work for you.

From that conversation to now, I have faithfully taken my medicine as prescribed and have included prayer, studying the bible, devotional reading of the Bible, meditation on God, exercising, eating properly, and rest as my treatment. I have also implemented healthy connections with others and thinking. I make it a point to start off with forgiveness, rather it is towards others or myself, and I have people in my circle that hold me accountable. These principles have served to be what has helped me in my recovery process.

In 2015 I finally completed all of the prerequisites for my dental hygiene degree and was accepted into the hygiene program in 2017; This was such a weight off of my shoulder! Even though I was going to school year after year; and over- coming barrier after barrier; because it was such a long time period of my life, I had gotten to the point that I was taken classes and I had lost sight of ever earning my degree.

I grew up believing that higher education was a realistic goal for myself, and despite having a mental health condition; I never knew that it would make it harder to accomplish my goal of earning my degree. One year of school turned into twenty-five years of trying to complete a two-year degree. I needed school, it was a positive redirection in my life; it allowed me to never stop trying to rise above the poverty that was all around me; in fact, my debilitating condition suggested that I should ball up in a fetal position and throw in the towel; but I refused to give up.

Each time I had a break down, I would have to overcome the physical, and cognitive obstacles that took months and at times years to bounce back from. There have been many layers to my recovery process; and there will always be aspects of my care that take different shape and it is dependent upon what is going on in my life. Often, I would experience the outside situational influences of life affecting me negatively on the inside. I had to learn how to care for myself and do what was best for me.

I have found that I have done well with learning how to talk about what I'm feeling and reading up on concepts that aide me with understanding how to sort through difficulties. I had to learn that emotions are neither bad nor good; but it's how you express the emotions that make them bad, or good.

There have been situations in my life that rendered me speechless, and not knowing how to emote properly; yet in those times, I tried to get a good night of rest; to then face the new day. Afterwhile, I got passed the hard part; and I was alive; so, for me, I'm here and it's time to openly discuss my experience.

When I finally got accept into my dental hygiene program, I had painted myself in a corner, and I no longer had the desire to complete my degree. I decided to go a different route. I wanted to become a landlord, and possible manage multiple properties; so, I bought my first house.

Once I let go of school, the floodgate opened, and I started to advance financially on a level that I had never seen before! I was able to balance my life to the point of reentering the workforce, and for the first time in my life; I had gotten to the point of being gainfully employed.

Let me say this, it hasn't been easy, and I have to take more mental health breaks than the average person; but I'm able to maintain a job. In fact, I have been functioning on a consistent stable level and haven't been in the hospital for a breakdown in almost 15 years.

In the black community (black churches and poorer neighborhoods), it is harder for trust to be established with the medical community due to various issues stemming back to slavery. As a black person, we have witness medical bias on such an extraordinarily high level; we have had issues with being misinformed, not informed and down- right handled wrong. There is no wonder that at times, it takes longer for us to educate ourselves, so, we may be able to make an informed decision about our care.

It is time out for allowing others to make health choices for us, there are many resources available to help bridge the gap within taking care of ourselves. We cannot continue to neglect our health and expect to live a longer life. Ignorance of a thang is not acceptable, get involved, take action and make the change that is needed. We must be held accountable for what we know and take measures to learn what we don't know. There is no shame in being informed, the dishonor comes in the lack of knowledge. We are in a technological age, and we are surrounded by so much information; for me, I will not go through life sticking my head in the sand.

Most of my treatment for my mental health condition, consisted of me sitting on the couch of self-help utilizing resources that I had to search out, nothing automatically came to me. I found that as I cared for myself, I had to continue the process; there wasn't nor will there be a time when I can kick back and forgo my care. I still have to deal with the stressors of life, and also situations that hurt to the core. There have been many enjoyable moments alone the path to my today, and I continue to forge forward trying to advocate for mental health wellness and awareness.

I tell my story with no regret, I have hope; and I want to help someone else. Perhaps, this will help someone come to the realization that they may need to seek professional help, or that their loved one may need assistance with navigating the mental health care system. I have a few words of wisdom to share: never be afraid to get help, it may take some time to find the right care, and never feel like you have to go through your situation alone.

I'm uncertain why it took me as long as it did for me to properly care for myself; it may have been due to me not seeing myself as what I viewed as needing on going mental health care; it also can be attributed to me being under educated on the subject matter. Nevertheless, once I began to learn all I could, and started to believe that mental health was a real part of everyone's life; I was empowered to share my experience.

In my opinion, it wasn't until the Coronavirus of 2019, that caring for mental health issues was widely accepted on a global level; people had to realize that the subject needed to be effectively addressed. Now more so than ever before, people are reaching out to get help and they are rising above the stigma that has hung over this condition for decades. I believe that there has been a negative connection to mental health care because of so many unknowns about the cause of such conditions.

I look forward to the day that anyone experiencing any sort of mental health crisis, would be able to talk about their condition, without prejudice. Most importantly, I hope that my story has given someone hope. What I have learned about mental health is due to my experience, what I have to share about the subject matter may save someone's life. When someone is in pain, and they can't help themselves; please step in and aide them. Help comes in various forms; you may be able to point someone in the direction of a resource that may benefit them, or you may be able to listen to someone that is in crisis. My prayer is that if you need help, please seek it out; if you can aide someone else; please do so without causing further harm.

CHAPTER 12

SUPPORT SYSTEM

W hen my life was interrupted with a mental health crisis, I did not go through that experience alone; my family, friends, church family, and my community went through the journey also. I thought it would be good to include expressions from those that were there to give an account of how they felt, what they witnessed and their initial thoughts; as they processed the event.

This is what my mother had to say:

"When ya'll came home from the show, ya'll were talking about it; I noticed you were acting kinda strange, strange like; talking to yourself. I thought you were on the phone talking to someone. I started praying, cause, I knew something was wrong. I started asking you questions, but you avoided answering me. I decided that I was going to take you back up to the club and have the man undo what he did, I didn't know that you had been hypnotized, until your sisters said what happen. I called your Aunt Vickie, told her what happen, and she came over the next day and we took you back to the club. I told the man he had to undo it. I didn't know what was going on with you. The man told us he couldn't do anything, so we left. You wouldn't sleep and you stop eating. For some apparent reason, you thought something was

wrong with the food and you threw it in the trash; I fried some chicken and you just put it all in the trash can. You wouldn't keep your clothes on, you were on your menstrual cycle and you kept taking off your pad and your clothes. I needed help with you because you were fighting me, so I called your godbrother Victor, and he had to come in the room and get you to put your clothes and pad on. You started fighting him, but he was able to get you to keep the stuff on. He called his mom in Arkansas, and asked her to pray for you, she called the other prayer warriors and they started calling on God for you. Grandma Dolly had made an appointment with this Mexican spiritualist lady at her job, and when we were on our way there; the Lord told me that if I took you to her, you would be worse off; so, I changed my mind about that. You were in a bad way, and I was scared. I knew I couldn't do anything but pray, and I was praying. We knew we had to call for help when you hit me, you would never try to hurt me; when the squad came to take you to the hospital, it took all six of us that were there to get you in the restraints and into the ambulance. I knew that only God could help you, and He helped me to understand what was wrong with you."

One of my childhood friends that attended Israelite Church of God in Christ, in San Diego, CA, with me had this to say:

"How I felt when Ticha first got sick; I felt shocked, surprised, sad, and mad. All these emotions, all put together...then I had so many questions like: How did this happen to someone like her? Not Ticha, she is my friend...she has a supportive family, her friends and family love her! Could anybody see the signs? Why? All I could do at the time was pray for her, but in my heart, I knew that she would be ok. It was 1990, we sort of lost contact, but she was always in my heart. When I found out that she was in the hospital, I did not know how but I knew I wanted to see her. I remember driving up to the hospital with one of our high school friends (that attended church with us), *we walked in, and we saw her mom sitting outside Ticha's room. She was probably praying. Ticha's momma was a praying woman. Before we entered the room, she wanted to mentally prepare us because, the girl we knew was not the girl we were about to see. However, as we approached, she was so happy to see friends coming to visit. Through this ordeal, Ticha had lost so many people that she called friend. One moment I will always remember about that night is, if I ever witnessed a woman of faith, I saw it in her mom's face. Despite what the many doctors said, and she never gave up on Ticha being completely restored. Her mom was right, who we saw that night, was not the girl I grew up with. I was just glad I had the chance to see her. She did not recognize me. She just kept repeating the same word over*

and over "popcorn," "popcorn." My friend and I just laughed and sat in the room with her for about 20 to 30 minutes. In that stage of my life, I did not really engage in prayer enough to pray for her or the room she was occupying. I knew she was in good hands because of the faith of her momma. I did not get a chance to see her anymore, but I continuously asked about her and would say a prayer and believe that I would see her again."

This is what my older middle sister had to say:

"When, or what started me to think something was wrong with you was when the show was over, and the hypnotist was touching everyone that he had put under hypnosis; you were at the end of the line, and he didn't come and touch you. I was thinking, hey he didn't come touch Ticha. Then a few days passed, and I got word that you were acting strange. You were acting out the different characters that the hypnotist had you doing during the show. One minute you were acting like a robot, then a valley girl. You were mumbling and we couldn't understand what you were saying. I was saying this isn't normal she is acting strange. When you had your full episode, I was at my house with my family, and I came over. You were combative, and you started fighting our godbrother. You were in your room when I walked inside, and I was trying to calm you down; you were aggressive and

you kept saying, "we got to save the children, all of them," we didn't know what you were talking about. You were not yourself. When you finally went to the hospital, they had you on so much medicine, and you were moving slow and talking really slow. It was so sad, and scary; I wouldn't want anyone to go through what you did. To be out of your mind and not know who any of us were; it still makes me emotional and tear up thinking about it. You kept telling us that you were ready to leave the hospital and go home with us; that would make me break down and cry, because we couldn't take you home. You had only been in the hospital a day and it was too early for you to come home; you still were out of it and needed to get better. That was hard to watch you beg to go home, and we couldn't take you home. That broke my heart. There was nothing we could do to make it better for you, we were helpless. I truly thank God for bringing you through, and for the woman you are today; you are my superhero and my inspiration, and you always will be."

This is what one of my close prayer partners had to say when he came to visit me in the hospital when I had the breakdown in 2007:

"What I remember most vividly is how I felt being at the hospital unable to reach you. I was sad, eager and a bit anxious to help, but frustrated because I couldn't reach you... You were unreachable (in many ways) and all I could do

was pray, be present with your family, and let God continue to work through the process. I felt a bit helpless...there was a sharp sense that this was out of my hands (as well as out of the hands of those closest to you, like your mother). When I entered the hospital, your ex-husband was blocking even your mother from seeing you, then of course the medical facilities were protecting you, and lastly you weren't yet coherent...so I adjusted and realized it would just take some time before you were reachable again. There was a process of repair you had to go through in order to be reachable again."

My son had this to say about the situation:

"I was young, it was new to me and I didn't understand it; it was new to all of us and nobody understood. I was trying to figure it out. I had to stay at my granny's house, and I didn't know why I had to be over there all the time. No one told me why I would need to be there. I was just over there. Then it became a routine over the times you got sick. What made it better, or not better; smoother was, the support we had from everyone. It wasn't just you and me going through it, everyone was there too. That made it easier to go through. It wasn't just us out there, it could have been a lot worse; if it was just us out there it would have been harder. Thank God it was the way it was, and it happened for a reason. I noticed when I was a kid, the intelligence I had; I *could tell things about people. I would pay attention to the way a person's eyes looked, and the way they were moving; and I could tell what was going on with them. I pay attention to things that most people never notice about people. I can understand things, without someone telling me about it. Seeing it, I can tell that something is going on; even if I don't know what it is, I can tell that something is wrong. Being patient, I pick up on things; a person's body language, the way they talking; that's what I learned when I was young. Watching a person's demeanor and picking up on things about a person; I have always been really good with that since I was a kid. When I was young and we lived in California, I was taught to pay attention to people, and my surroundings. Even now, I can sense something about someone without them saying anything to me or anyone telling me about them. A person's eyes would always let me know about them. I would coach myself to pay attention, breath, and calm down; especially if I was scared or something. I would teach myself to slow my heart down, and when there would be trouble or something; when I would do this, it would make the situation not as bad as I thought it would be, I would stay calm and pay attention. I learned self- control and that helped me. When you had the breakdowns, they were at different time points and scattered. I was trying to see what caused them to happen, and I wondered to myself why it happened. I guess you were going through different things, and I was trying to figure out the cause. I guess I never understood that, and I always wonder why, and how? Different points of your life I guess more things are on your mind, it's kind of like; when you know that you are great on the inside, and you're doing the right things. You're working hard, and doing what you're supposed to do, and it's right there. You know it's right there cause you been putting in the work. We are not patient enough, cause we want it now, sometimes people have breakdowns about that, cause people just want to be great. Sometimes you not seeing it happen fast enough, the level up steps; and you can have an emotional breakdown, because of the frustration. I think it's a part of frustration, and you overwhelm yourself, you know from trying to reach your dreams of what you want to be. So, you over work yourself, and overheat...something like that. Everyone would always say that you would be okay, you just sick right now; it was passive. People didn't have enough information on it, so that's all they would say; and told me to pray. It wasn't like now where you can google it and have the information about it or watch a video."*

This is what one of my closest friends in the ministry had to say about my 2007 episode:

"I remember the Sunday before it happened, we were sitting together in the evening service and I felt like something wasn't quite right, but I didn't know what. You seemed agitated and you were behaving in a way that was out of character for you. After the service one of the saints, the one that was called on to minister confronted me because they thought that we were disrupting or something during the service. They really didn't understand what was happening and they put their own spin on what they thought was going on, and I didn't go into any details with them or explain anything to them; I just apologized for offending them and let it go. Later that week, it was a Wednesday; your mom called me and I was at work in the clinic. I could remember just sitting on the floor in the clinic listening to your mom explain what was going on. She shared how frustrated she and your family were because she felt like Steve was trying to limit their access to you and their involvement with your care. I remember feeling helpless and kind of paralyzed, and frustrated; because I knew something was wrong, but there wasn't anything that I could do; other than pray. Even though I know that prayer is powerful, it just didn't feel like it was enough in that moment. Later that night in bible study, Elder Seth came over to me and we encouraged each other and agreed to do what we do for each other; all three of us, which is to touch and agree in prayer. Despite having some

experience with mental health issues professionally, this was the first time experiencing this with someone of whom I have a personal relationship with. I was anxious and frustrated because I just wanted to know that you would be okay. I can remember the first time I talked with you after you were released from the hospital, and you sounded so fragile. I remember being so concerned about what to say, because I didn't want to say the wrong thing. I also wanted you to know, because at the time this happened, we hadn't been friends that long; but I wanted you to know that I was there for you, if you needed me. You were pretty candid and upfront about what happened, and that put me at ease. When we got off the phone, I knew that you would be okay; and the Lord would carry you. It has been a blessing to watch you grow and incorporate your experience, into a powerful testimony that you have used to propel you into advocacy for people that experience mental health challenges."

One of the centralized themes from everyone that witnessed me go through my breakdowns, was an overwhelming feeling of helplessness. I am thankful that I didn't go through this painful experience alone. I have been very fortunate to have people in my circle that truly love and care about me. It's one thing to feel alone, and it is a whole other thing to actually be alone. I know that sticking by someone's side during their time of need is key to anyone having a chance at properly overcoming the psychological residue from any traumatic event.

Imagine the millions of people that go through mental health crisis without a solid support system. Where is their help? Where is their voice? How can we empower others to be that support that brings hope to someone in need?

It may take for someone to gain the courage to make a difference within how they may be able to spread the word and offer themselves as an aide for someone needing assistance. One of the main ingredients to me becoming mentally stronger, was other people helping me, when I couldn't help myself. For this reason, I am determined to speak up for Mental health awareness.

No one has all of the answers, however if we ensure that we all do our part, we can change the way in which we perceive and approach the mental health care system. What I went through was full of torment, there were many days that were foggy, and caused me to be unable to see in front of me. I couldn't see passed the crisis, nor what my fate would be. As time passed, I grew stronger, and made adjustments with my care; when I did that, I could see myself waving goodbye to every barrier that blocked my path. My pathway is clear, and the fog is gone. No more torment from mental health, my strength remains because I speak out. My journey has meaning and nothing I went through will be in vain, I will continue to share my experience and bring light to a dark subject.

If you or someone you know are in need of help, you may contact your local medical provider or local listing for assistance. Here is a list of organizations that help people when they are in need:

NAMI, the National Alliance on Mental Illness; *https://nami.org*

NIH, National Institute of Mental Health; *https://nimh.nih.gov*

SAMHSA, Substance Abuse and Mental Health Services; *https://www.samhsa.gov*

National Suicide Prevention Lifeline; *https://suicidepreventionlifeline.org*

Veterans Crisis Line; *https://www.veteranscrisisline.net*

Made in USA - Kendallville, IN
37015_9798985229707
12 20 2021 1846